CSS3 Quick Syntax Reference

A Pocket Guide to the Cascading Style Sheets Language

Second Edition

Mikael Olsson

Apress®

CSS3 Quick Syntax Reference: A Pocket Guide to the Cascading Style Sheets Language

Mikael Olsson
Hammarland, Finland

ISBN-13 (pbk): 978-1-4842-4902-4   ISBN-13 (electronic): 978-1-4842-4903-1
https://doi.org/10.1007/978-1-4842-4903-1

Managing Director, Apress Media LLC: Welmoed Spahr
Acquisitions Editor: Steve Anglin
Development Editor: Matthew Moodie
Coordinating Editor: Mark Powers

Cover designed by eStudioCalamar

Cover image designed by Freepik (www.freepik.com)

Distributed to the book trade worldwide by Springer Science+Business Media New York, 233 Spring Street, 6th Floor, New York, NY 10013. Phone 1-800-SPRINGER, fax (201) 348-4505, e-mail orders-ny@springer-sbm.com, or visit www.springeronline.com. Apress Media, LLC is a California LLC and the sole member (owner) is Springer Science + Business Media Finance Inc (SSBM Finance Inc). SSBM Finance Inc is a **Delaware** corporation.

For information on translations, please e-mail editorial@apress.com; for reprint, paperback, or audio rights, please email bookpermissions@springernature.com.

Apress titles may be purchased in bulk for academic, corporate, or promotional use. eBook versions and licenses are also available for most titles. For more information, reference our Print and eBook Bulk Sales web page at http://www.apress.com/bulk-sales.

Any source code or other supplementary material referenced by the author in this book is available to readers on GitHub via the book's product page, located at www.apress.com/9781484249024. For more detailed information, please visit http://www.apress.com/source-code.

Printed on acid-free paper

Table of Contents

About the Author

Mikael Olsson is a professional programmer, web entrepreneur, and author. He works for an R&D company in Finland, at which he specializes in software development. In his spare time, he writes books and creates web sites that summarize various fields of interest. The books Mikael writes are focused on teaching their subjects in the most efficient way possible, by explaining only what is relevant and practical without any unnecessary repetition or theory. The portal to his online businesses and other web sites is www.siforia.com.

About the Technical Reviewer

Victor Sumner is a Senior Software Engineer at Desire2Learn Inc., helping to build and maintain an integrated learning platform. As a self-taught developer, he is always interested in emerging technologies and enjoys working on and solving problems that are outside his comfort zone.

When not at the office, Victor has a number of hobbies, including photography, horseback riding, and gaming. He lives in Ontario, Canada, with his wife, Alicia, and their two children.

Introduction

CSS, which stands for Cascading Style Sheets, is a stylistic language that defines how web pages are presented. It complements HTML, which is the language used for describing the structure of web site content. Because HTML predates CSS, it includes a number of limited stylistic elements and attributes, but they have largely been deprecated in favor of the much greater design control offered by CSS.

One of the main features of CSS is that it enables the complete separation of a web site's presentation from its content. This separation reduces the complexity and repetition associated with including stylistic information in the structural content. Furthermore, this separation makes it easy to enforce site-wide consistency in the presentation of a web site because the entire look and feel of a site can be controlled from a single style sheet document.

As one of the core languages of the Web, CSS is used today by almost all web sites to enhance the web experience. It has been a revolution in the World Wide Web and is a must-learn language for anyone working with web design. Like HTML, the CSS language is easy to learn and use, as is shown in this book.

CSS Versions

The CSS language is under ongoing development by the World Wide Web Consortium (W3C), which is the international standards organization for the Internet. The W3C writes the specifications that web browsers implement to display web pages consistently in compliance with those specifications. Each new specification extends the language with new features while maintaining backward compatibility.

The first specification, CSS level 1 (or CSS 1), became a W3C recommendation in 1996. In 1998, CSS 2 was finalized, extending CSS 1 with additional features. Because all widely used web browsers currently implement the features of both these specifications, it is seldom necessary to make a distinction between them, and this book does so only when relevant.

Since 1998, the W3C has been working on CSS 3. Unlike the two earlier levels of CSS, this level became considerably larger and was therefore split into several separate specifications called modules. This split allowed the modules to mature independently at their own pace. As a result of the ongoing development, support for CSS 3 varies. Some features are stable and have widespread browser support; other features are supported only by the latest browser versions or are not supported at all. This book focuses mainly on the CSS 3 features that are supported in the major browsers at the time of writing.

Rule Structure

CSS is commonly used within a style sheet document, which consists of a list of rules. For example, a rule to color all paragraph elements red is shown here:

```
p { color: red; }
```

This rule has two parts: a selector and a declaration block. The selector is the link between the HTML document and the style sheet that specifies the element to which the rule is applied. In this case, it is the type selector p that applies to all paragraph elements (<p>). Any HTML element can be used as a type selector in this way.

The declaration block, which is enclosed within curly braces, defines the styling applied to the selected elements. The block can contain one or more declarations, each of which is made up of a style property followed by a colon and a valid value for that property. Each declaration is terminated with a semicolon, although this is optional for the last one.

```
p { color: red; background: black }
```

Although the last semicolon is not necessary, it is a good practice to include it because it is easy to forget the missing semicolon when you add more styles to the rule. Another general practice is to use lowercase letters when writing CSS, even though selectors and properties are case insensitive.

To summarize, a style rule consists of a selector and one or more declarations, each comprising one or more property-value pairs. This structure is illustrated here:

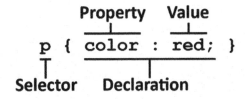

CHAPTER 1

Using CSS

There are three ways to insert CSS into an HTML document: by using an internal style sheet, inline styles, or an external style sheet. An internal style sheet applies to a single page, an inline style to a single element, and an external style sheet to potentially an entire web site.

Internal Style Sheet

An internal style sheet is useful when a single document needs to have its own unique styling. The style sheet is then embedded within the `<head>` section of the web document using the `<style>` element. This element is a container for style sheet rules and should have its type attribute set to `"text/css"`.

```
<style type="text/css">
  p { color: red; }
</style>
```

Inline Style

Styling can be assigned to an individual element by using the `style` attribute to set an inline style. It is a generic attribute that can be included in any HTML start tag, and its value is the CSS declarations that will be applied to the element, separated by semicolons. There is no need to specify a selector because the declarations implicitly belong to the current element.

```
<p style="color: green">Green text</p>
```

© Mikael Olsson 2019
M. Olsson, *CSS3 Quick Syntax Reference*, https://doi.org/10.1007/978-1-4842-4903-1_1

This approach should be used sparingly because it mixes style with content and therefore makes future changes more cumbersome. It can be useful as a quick way to test styles before they are moved out to an external style sheet.

External Style Sheet

The most common way to include CSS is through an external style sheet. The style sheet rules are placed in a separate text file with a `.css` file extension. This style sheet is then referenced using the `<link>` element in the web page header. The `rel` (relationship) attribute must be set to `"stylesheet"` and the meta `type` attribute can optionally be set to `"text/css"`. The location of the style sheet is specified with the `href` attribute.

```
<link rel="stylesheet" type="text/css" href="MyStyle.css">
```

Another less common way to include an external style sheet is to use the CSS `@import` function from inside of the `<style>` element. For this function to work, it must be placed before any other rules.

```
<style type="text/css">
 @import url(MyStyle.css);
</style>
```

Using an external style sheet is often preferred because it completely separates CSS from the HTML document. It is then possible to quickly create a consistent look for an entire web site and to change its appearance just by editing a single CSS document. It also has performance benefits because external style sheets are cached and therefore need to be downloaded only once—for the first page a visitor views at your site.

Testing Environment

To experiment with CSS, you can use a simple text editor such as Notepad in Windows or TextEdit on a Mac. Type the following single style rule into a new document in the editor. The rule will color the background of a web document red.

```
body { background: red; }
```

Save the file as "MyStyle.css" and then open another empty document. This new document will become the HTML file that uses the external style sheet you just created. Write the following HTML markup into the document, which includes a reference to the style sheet along with the minimal markup for a HTML 5 web document:

```
<!DOCTYPE html>
<html>
  <head>
    <meta charset="UTF-8">
    <title>Example</title>
    <link rel="stylesheet" href="MyStyle.css">
  </head>
  <body>
    <p>This page is red</p>
  </body>
</html>
```

Go ahead and save this text file as "MyPage.html" in the same folder as the CSS file. You have now created a simple environment in which you can test CSS. To view the page, open MyPage.html with your web browser. You will see that the background is indeed colored red because of the rule in the style sheet.

View Source

While you have the browser opened, you can view the HTML markup that makes up the page by pressing Ctrl+U on a PC or Cmd+U on a Mac. This shortcut works in all major browsers, including Chrome, Firefox, Safari, Opera, Edge, and Internet Explorer (IE). You can also find the view source window by right-clicking on the page and selecting "View Source." In Firefox and Chrome, the style sheet is clickable, allowing you to view the external style sheet rules that apply to the web page.

Viewing the source code of web pages like this provides a great way to learn from other web developers. Whenever you find an interesting element on a web page—whether it is created with HTML, CSS or JavaScript—the page source will reveal how it was created.

Comments

Comments in CSS are created by using the C-style notation (/* */). Everything placed between /* and */ will be ignored by browsers, even if the delimiters span multiple lines.

```
/* Multi-line
   Comment */
```

The main use of comments is to clarify the code to developers, including you in the future. They can also be used to improve readability by delimiting sections of the style sheet or providing meta data about the file, such as the author's name.

```
/*
 * Meta data
 */
```

```
/*** Section heading ***/

p { margin-top: -1px; } /* clarification */
```

Comments are also useful for temporarily deactivating declarations or entire style rules for testing purposes.

```
p { /* color: white; */ }
```

Whitespace

Whitespace refers to spaces, tabs, and new lines. You are free to format your style sheets however you like with whitespace to make them easier to read. One common formatting convention is to split declarations across multiple lines.

```
.fruit {
  color: red;
  margin: 1px;
}
```

Another popular convention is to keep a rule's declarations in a single line and split the declarations into multiple lines only when they become too numerous.

```
.fruit       { color: red;    margin: 1px; }
.fruit.apple { color: green; margin: 2px; }
```

The formatting you use is a matter of preference. Choose the one that makes sense to you and aim to keep it consistent.

CHAPTER 2

Grouping

To keep style sheets short and easy to edit, similar rules can be grouped together. This grouping provides several ways to specify a set of related rules. For example, you can color the text red and the background black for two header elements in four different ways, as described in the following sections.

Ungrouped Rules

Each rule can be written separately, which allows you to apply individual style rules to each selected element.

```
h1 { color: red; }
h1 { background: black; }
h2 { color: red; }
h2 { background: black; }
```

Grouped Selectors

The selectors can be grouped together by separating them with a comma. This will apply the declaration to both selectors.

```
h1, h2 { color: red; }
h1, h2 { background: black; }
```

© Mikael Olsson 2019
M. Olsson, *CSS3 Quick Syntax Reference*, https://doi.org/10.1007/978-1-4842-4903-1_2

Grouped Declarations

The declarations can be grouped together by separating them with a semicolon. All styles within the declaration block will be applied to the selector.

```
h1 {
  color: red;
  background: black;
}
h2 {
  color: red;
  background: black;
}
```

Grouped Selectors and Declarations

Both the selectors and declarations can be combined, resulting in a single rule. This method offers the most concise way to write these rules.

```
h1, h2 {
  color: red;
  background: black;
}
```

Rules should be grouped whenever possible to make the style sheet more succinct. This has a small performance benefit because concise rules reduce the size of the style sheet, which makes the CSS file load more quickly. Moreover, it is convenient to specify the properties in only one place, in case they have to be changed later. Additionally, grouping selectors with similar styles makes it easier to maintain consistency between them.

CHAPTER 3

Class and ID Selectors

Class and id selectors define rules that apply to only a selected set of HTML elements. They allow you to identify individual elements, or groups of elements, without having to style all instances of the element type.

Class Selector

The class selector is used to identify a group of elements. It is recognized by the period sign (.), followed by a class name. A general class is defined here, which can be applied to any element.

```
/* Selects any element with class name myclass */
.myclass {}
```

The selector can also be a specific class that can be applied to only one type of element. Such a class is defined by declaring the element's name before the period sign.

```
/* Selects any <p> element with class name myclass */
p.myclass {}
```

Specific classes make it easier to identify where a class is used, whereas general classes can allow for greater code reuse.

© Mikael Olsson 2019
M. Olsson, *CSS3 Quick Syntax Reference*, https://doi.org/10.1007/978-1-4842-4903-1_3

Class Example

Suppose that the text inside of some elements should be colored, but not for all instances of those elements. The first step then is to add a general class rule with a color property specified.

```
.info { color: green; }
```

This rule says that any element whose `class` attribute has the value of `"info"` will have this style.

```
<p class="info">Green</p>
```

If a class rule will be used by only a single element type, it can instead be defined as a specific class. Doing so makes it easier for anyone reading the style sheet to understand where the style is used.

```
p.warn { color: orange; }
```

A specific class rule is applied to the document in the same way as a general class rule, but it will style elements of only the specified type.

```
<p class="warn">Orange</p>
```

More than one class rule can be applied to a single element by separating each class name with a space. This makes class rules very versatile.

```
<p class="style1 style2"></p>
```

ID Selector

The id selector is used to identify a single unique element. It works much like the class selector, but uses a pound sign (#) instead of a period and the `id` attribute instead of the `class` attribute. Like the `class` attribute, `id` is a generic attribute that can be applied to virtually any HTML element. It provides a unique identifier for an element within a document.

```
/* Selects the element with id set to myid */
#myid {}
```

Like class selectors, id selectors can be qualified with an element. However, because there should be only one element with a given id, this additional qualifier is considered unnecessary.

```
/* Selects the <p> element with id set to myid */
p#myid {}
```

ID Example

The following id selector will match the one and only element in the document whose id attribute is set to that id. This selector can therefore be used instead of the class selector if a style is intended to be applied to only a single element instance.

```
#err { color: red; }
```

An id rule is applied to an element using the id attribute. Because the id attribute has to be unique, each id selector can be used on only one element per web page. Therefore, the id selector implicitly specifies that the style is used only once on any one page.

```
<p id="err">Red</p>
```

Class and ID Guidelines

In many instances, using classes is the preferred method of selecting elements in CSS because classes are both flexible and reusable. Ids, on the other hand, are often used for structural elements of a site, such as #content and #footer, to highlight that those elements serve a unique role.

CHAPTER 4

Attribute Selectors

Attribute selectors allow style to be added to elements based on their attributes and attribute values.

Attribute Selector

Elements that use a specific attribute can be matched using the attribute selector. This selector does not take the value of the attribute into account.

```
input[type] {}
```

This selector will match only input elements that use the `type` attribute, such as the following element:

```
<input type="text">
```

Attribute Value Selector

Both attribute and value can be matched using the attribute value selector.

```
input[type="submit"] {}
```

Input elements that have their `type` attribute set to `submit` will be matched by this rule, as in the following example:

```
<input type="submit">
```

© Mikael Olsson 2019
M. Olsson, *CSS3 Quick Syntax Reference*, https://doi.org/10.1007/978-1-4842-4903-1_4

Language Attribute Selector

The language attribute selector is used to match the lang attribute.

```
p[lang|="en"] {}
```

This selector will match any elements whose lang attribute value begins with "en", such as "en-US". Note that language codes such as these are case insensitive.

```
<p lang="en">English</p>
<p lang="en-US">American English</p>
```

Delimited Value Selector

The [attribute~=value] selector will apply to elements whose attribute value contains the given word among a space-separated list of words.

```
input[value~="word"] {}
```

This rule will select both of the following elements. The word needs to be an exact case-sensitive match, so the selector will not apply to, for instance, "Word" or "words".

```
<input type="text" value="word">
<input type="text" value="word word2">
```

Value Substring Selector

The [attribute*=value] selector matches elements whose attribute value contains the specified substring.

```
p[title*="para"] {}
```

Paragraph elements with a `title` containing "para" will be matched by this rule.

```
<p title="my paragraph"></p>
```

Value Start Selector

The `[attribute^=value]` selector matches every element whose attribute value begins with the specified string.

```
p[title^="first"] {}
```

Paragraphs with a `title` value starting with "first" will have this rule applied.

```
<p title="first paragraph"></p>
```

Value End Selector

The `[attribute$=value]` selector matches an element if its attribute value ends with the specified string.

```
p[title$="1"] {}
```

In the following markup, the value of the `title` attribute ends with "1" and will therefore be matched by this rule.

```
<p title="paragraph 1"></p>
```

CHAPTER 5

Pseudo Selectors

The pseudo-classes and pseudo-elements are keywords that can be appended to selectors to make them more specific. They are easy to recognize because they are always preceded by one or two colons.

Pseudo-Elements

Pseudo-elements enable parts of an element to be styled. Only one of these can be applied to any one selector.

first-letter and first-line

The pseudo-elements ::first-letter and ::first-line can apply styles to the first letter and the first line of an element. They work only on block elements such as paragraphs.

```
p::first-letter { font-size: 120%; }
p::first-line { font-weight: bold; }
```

The preceding first rule makes the initial letter in a paragraph render 20% larger than other text. The second rule makes the first line of text in a paragraph bold.

© Mikael Olsson 2019
M. Olsson, *CSS3 Quick Syntax Reference*, https://doi.org/10.1007/978-1-4842-4903-1_5

before and after

As their names indicate, the `::before` and `::after` pseudo-elements can target the location before and after an element. They are used together with the `content` property to insert content before or after an element.

```
p::before { content: "Before"; }
p::after { content: "After"; }
```

These rules make the following paragraph display as "BeforeMiddleAfter":

```
<p>Middle</p>
```

The `content` property is special in that it can be used only together with these two pseudo-elements. It is also the only property that breaks the line between content (HTML) and design (CSS). Keep in mind that this line should be broken only when the presence of a piece of content comes down to a design decision. For example, the `content` property can be used to add an icon before an element, which can be done using the `url` function.

```
p.bullet::before { content: url(my-bullet.png); }
```

The four pseudo-elements described so far were introduced in CSS 2 where they used only a single colon (`:`). CSS 3 introduced the double-colon (`::`) notation to differentiate pseudo-elements from pseudo-classes. W3C has deprecated use of the single colon notation, but all major browsers continue to support both syntaxes. Inclusion of the single colon notation would be appropriate only if support for the legacy browser IE8 is desired.

```
.foo:after {}  /* CSS 2 */
.foo::after {} /* CSS 3 */
```

All major desktop browsers support a fifth pseudo-element –
::selection. As the name implies, this pseudo-element can add styling to
content selected by the user. Valid styling properties for most browsers are
limited to color and background-color.

```
::selection { background-color: blue; }
```

Pseudo-Classes

Pseudo-classes permit styling based on element relationships and on
information not found in the HTML document. Most of them fall into three
categories: dynamic, structural, and user interface pseudo-classes. Unlike
pseudo-elements, multiple pseudo-classes can be applied to a selector to
make it even more specific.

Dynamic Pseudo-Classes

The first category of pseudo-classes is used to apply styles to links or other
interactive elements when their state is changed. There are five of them, all
of which were introduced in CSS 2.

link and visited

The dynamic pseudo-classes :link and :visited can be applied only to
the anchor element (<a>). The :link pseudo-class matches links to pages
that have not been viewed, whereas :visited matches links that have
been viewed.

```
a:link {}    /* unvisited links */
a:visited {} /* visited links */
```

active and hover

Another pseudo-class is :active, which matches elements as they are being activated, for example by a mouse click. This is most useful for styling anchor elements, but it can be applied to any element.

```
a:active {} /* activated links */
```

A selector with the :hover pseudo-class appended to it is applied when the user moves a pointing device, such as a mouse, over the selected element. It is popularly used to create link roll-over effects.

```
a:hover {} /* hovered links */
```

These four pseudo-classes need to appear in the proper order when applied to the same selector. Specifically, the :hover pseudo-class must come after :link and :visited, and for :active to work it must appear after :hover. The phrase "love and hate" can be used as a reminder for the initial letters that make up the correct order.

```
a:link     {} /* L */
a:visited {} /* V */
a:hover    {} /* H */
a:active   {} /* A */
```

focus

The last dynamic pseudo-class is :focus, which can be used on elements that can receive focus, such as the form <input> element. The difference between :active and :focus is that :active lasts only for the duration of the click, whereas :focus lasts until the element loses focus.

```
input:focus {}
```

Structural Pseudo-Classes

The structural pseudo-classes target elements based on their relation with other elements. CSS 2 included only one structural pseudo-class in this category, :first-child, whereas CSS 3 introduced a wide array of new ones. The CSS 3 structural pseudo-classes are supported in all major browsers.

first-child

The :first-child pseudo-class matches the first child of the selected element.

```
p:first-child {} /* first paragraph child */
```

In the following example, this rule applies to the first child element of the paragraph.

```
<p>
  <span>First child</span>
  <span>Text</span>
</p>
```

last-child

The :last-child pseudo-class represents the last child of the selected element.

```
p:last-child {} /* last paragraph child */
```

This rule targets the last child of the following paragraph element.

```
<p>
  <em>Text</em>
  <em>Last child</em>
</p>
```

only-child

The `:only-child` pseudo-class matches elements that do not have any siblings.

```
p:only-child {} /* children without siblings */
```

This rule is applied to the following first `<strong>` element because it is the only child of the paragraph. The second paragraph element has two children, so none of them are targeted by this rule.

```
<p>
  <strong>Only child</strong>
</p>

<p>
  <strong>Text</strong>
  <em>Text</em>
</p>
```

only-of-type

As its name implies, the `:only-of-type` selector matches the selected element only if it does not have any siblings of the same type.

```
p:only-of-type {} /* only <p> element */
```

The following paragraph is targeted by this rule because it is the only paragraph element of its parent.

```
<div>
  <h1>Text</h1>
  <p>Only of type</p>
</div>
```

first-of-type

The :first-of-type pseudo-class matches the first child element that is of the selected type.

```
p:first-of-type {} /* first <p> element */
```

It matches the first paragraph element in the following markup:

```
<div>
  <h1>Text</h1>
  <p>First of type</p>
  <p>Text</p>
</div>
```

last-of-type

The last sibling of a specific type can be selected with the :last-of-type pseudo-class.

```
strong:last-of-type {} /* last <strong> element */
```

This rule applies to the last <strong> element among its siblings.

```
<div>
  <strong>Text</strong>
  <strong>Last of type</strong>
</div>
```

nth-child

The :nth-child(an + b) pseudo-class matches every b child element after the children have been divided into groups of a elements.

```
p:nth-child(1)    {} /* first child */
p:nth-child(2n)   {} /* even children */
p:nth-child(2n+1) {} /* odd children */
```

23

These rules apply to the following HTML markup:

```
<p>
  <span>First and odd</span>
  <span>Even</span>
  <span>Odd</span>
</p>
```

Matching odd and even children is a common operation. To simplify this selection the keywords odd and even can also be used, for instance to match every other row in a table.

```
tr:nth-child(even) {} /* even table rows */
tr:nth-child(odd)  {} /* odd table rows */
```

As shown, the argument to :nth-child() can be an integer, the keywords even or odd, or an expression in the form of an+b. In the expression form, the keyword n is a counter that iterates through all child elements. The counter may be negative, in which case the iteration occurs backwards. This can be used to select a specific number of first children.

```
p:nth-child(-n+3) {} /* first three children */
```

The math and arguments used together with :nth-child() are also valid for the next three pseudo-classes, all of which start with :nth.

nth-of-type

The :nth-of-type(an+b) pseudo-class matches the bth element of the selected type after the siblings of that type have been divided into groups of a elements.

```
p:nth-of-type(2)    {} /* second paragraph sibling */
p:nth-of-type(2n)   {} /* even paragraph siblings */
p:nth-of-type(2n+1) {} /* odd paragraph siblings */
```

The behavior of this pseudo-class is similar to :nth-child, but it matches siblings of the same type of the specified element instead of matching children of the specified element.

```
<div>
  <em>Text</em>
  <p>Odd</p>
  <p>Second and even</p>
  <p>Odd</p>
</div>
```

Similar to the other :nth pseudo-classes, the keywords odd and even can be used to match siblings of the same type whose index is odd or even.

```
p:nth-of-type(even) {} /* even paragraph siblings */
p:nth-of-type(odd)  {} /* odd paragraph siblings */
```

nth-last-of-type

The :nth-last-of-type(an+b) pseudo-class matches the element of the selected type that has an+b elements of that same type after it. This behavior is equivalent to the :nth-of-type pseudo-class, except that elements are counted starting from the bottom instead of the top.

```
p:nth-last-of-type(3)    {} /* third last paragraph */
p:nth-last-of-type(-n+2) {} /* last two paragraphs */
```

These two rules apply to the following example. The <em> element is not counted because it is not of the specified type—in this case, paragraph.

```
<div>
  <p>Third last</p>
  <p>Last two</p>
  <p>Last two</p>
  <em>Text</em>
</div>
```

nth-last-child

The :nth-last-child(an+b) pseudo-class represents any element that has an+b siblings after it. Its behavior is the same as :nth-child, except that it starts with the bottom element instead of the top one.

```
p:nth-last-child(3)    {} /* third last child */
p:nth-last-child(-n+2) {} /* last two children */
```

These two rules apply to the child elements in the following example:

```
<div>
  <p>Third last</p>
  <p>Last two</p>
  <p>Last two</p>
</div>
```

empty

The :empty pseudo-class matches selected elements that do not have any content.

```
p:empty {} /* empty paragraphs */
```

An element is considered empty if it has no child elements, text, or whitespace except for comments. The preceding rule applies to the following two paragraphs:

```
<p></p>
<p><!-- also empty --></p>
```

root

The :root pseudo-class matches the topmost element in the document tree. In HTML documents, this is always the <html> element.

```
:root {} /* root element */
```

This pseudo-class is mainly useful when CSS is used with other languages, such as XML, in which the root element can vary.

User Interface Pseudo-Classes

CSS 3 introduced a number of user interface pseudo-classes that are used to style interactive elements based on their current state.

enabled and disabled

The :enabled and :disabled pseudo-classes match any element of the selected type that is either enabled or disabled. They apply only to interactive elements that can be in either an enabled or disabled state, such as form elements.

```
input:enabled  { background: green; }
input:disabled { background: red; }
```

The following form contains one enabled and one disabled input element, which are affected by these two rules:

```
<form>
  <input type="text" name="enabled">
  <input type="text" name="disabled" disabled>
</form>
```

checked

The :checked pseudo-class matches elements that are in a selected state. It can be used only on check box, radio button, and <option> elements.

```
input[type="checkbox"]:checked {}
```

This rule matches any check boxes that are selected on the web page.

```
<form>
  <input type="checkbox">
</form>
```

valid and invalid

The :valid and :invalid pseudo-classes are used to provide feedback to users when they are filling out forms. Modern browsers can perform a basic field validation based on the input type of a form element and, together with these pseudo-classes, the result can be used to style the input element.

```
input:valid   { background: green; }
input:invalid { background: red; }
```

Two fields are given here, one required and one optional. The first field remains invalid until an e-mail is entered into the field. The second field is optional and is therefore valid if left empty.

```
<form>
  <input type="email" required>
  <input type="email">
</form>
```

Note that these pseudo-classes are in no way a substitution for proper form validation, using JavaScript or PHP, for example. Browser support for these two pseudo-classes exists in Chrome 10+, Firefox 4+, Safari 5+, Opera 10+, and IE 10+.

required and optional

A form field with the required attribute set is matched by the :required pseudo-class. The related :optional pseudo-class does the opposite: it matches input elements that do not have the required attribute set.

```
input:required { color: red; }
input:optional { color: gray; }
```

The following form contains one required and one optional input element, which is targeted by the previous styles:

```
<form>
  <input type="email" required>
  <input type="url">
</form>
```

Like the :valid and :invalid pseudo-classes, support for :required and :optional exists in Chrome 10+, Firefox 4+, Safari 5+, Opera 10+, and IE 10+.

out-of-range and in-range

An input element can include the min and max attributes to define the range of legal values for that element. The out-of-range and in-range pseudo-classes can be applied to target input elements that are currently inside or outside of this specified range.

```
input:out-of-range { color: red; }
input:in-range { color: black; }
```

Support for both of these pseudo-classes was added in Chrome 53+, Firefox 50+, Safari 10.1+, Opera 40+, and Edge 13+. The following form shows two input fields using the min and max attributes.

```
<form>
  <input type="number" min="1" max="5">
  <input type="date" min="1900-01-01">
</form>
```

read-write and read-only

Input elements that include the read-only attribute cannot be edited. Such elements can be targeted using the read-only pseudo-class. In contrast, any element that can be edited can be selected with the read-write pseudo-class.

```
input:read-only { color: gray; }
input:-moz-read-only { color: gray; }
input:read-write { color: black; }
input:-moz-read-write { color: gray; }
```

These pseudo-classes are usable in Chrome 36+, Firefox 3+, Safari 4+, Opera 11.5+, and Edge 13+. The –moz– prefix is necessary for all versions of Firefox. The following markup shows how the read-only attribute is applied to a form input element.

```
<form>
  <input type="text" value="unavailable" readonly>
</form>
```

Other Pseudo-Classes

Some pseudo-classes do not fit into any of the earlier categories, namely the :target, :lang" :not pseudo-classes.

target

The :target pseudo-class can style an element that is targeted through an id link. It can be useful for highlighting a targeted section of the document.

```
:target { font-weight: bold; } /* targeted element */
```

When the following internal page link is followed, this rule is applied to the anchor element. The browser also scrolls down to that element.

```
<a href="#my-target" id="my-target">In page link</a>
```

lang

The pseudo-class :lang() matches elements determined to be in the language provided by the argument.

```
p:lang(en) {}
```

This pseudo-class applies to paragraph elements that are intended for an English audience, such as the following paragraph:

```
<p lang="en">English</p>
```

Note that the behavior of this pseudo-class is similar to the language attribute selector. The difference is that the :lang pseudo-class also matches elements if the language is set on an ancestor element, or in some other way such as through the page HTTP header or <meta> tag.

```
<body lang="fr">
  <p>French</p>
</body>
```

not

The negation pseudo-class :not matches elements that are not targeted by the specified selector.

```
p:not(.first) { font-weight: bold; }
```

This example rule selects paragraphs that are not using the first class.

```
<p class="first">Not bold</p>
<p>Bold</p>
```

CHAPTER 6

Relationship Selectors

Relationship selectors match elements based on their relation with other elements. To understand these selectors, it is important to recognize how elements in a web document are related to each other.

HTML Hierarchy

An HTML document can be visualized as a tree with the `<html>` element as the root. Each element fits somewhere on this tree, and every element is either a parent or a child of another element. Any element above another one is called an ancestor, and the element directly above is the parent. Similarly, an element below another one is called a descendant, and the one directly below is a child. In turn, an element sharing the same parent as another element is called a sibling. Consider the following simple HTML 5 document:

```
<!DOCTYPE html>
<html>
  <head>
    <meta charset="UTF-8">
    <title>Example</title>
  </head>
```

```
<body>
  <h1>Heading</h1>
  <p>Paragraph</p>
</body>
</html>
```

In this example, `<h1>` and `<p>` are sibling elements because they share the same parent. Their parent element is `<body>`, and together with `<html>`, they are both ancestors to the sibling elements. In turn, the two sibling elements are child elements of `<body>` and descendants of both `<body>` and `<html>`. The hierarchy of this simple document is illustrated in Figure 6-1.

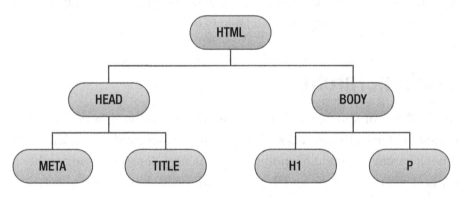

Figure 6-1. *Example HTML hierarchy*

Inheritance

Inheritance is another important concept in CSS. It makes certain styles apply not only to the specified element but also to all its descendant elements. For example, the `color` property is inherited by default, whereas the `border` property is not. This is usually the intended behavior, making inheritance very intuitive to use. Any property can explicitly be given the value inherit to use the same value as the one the parent element has for that property.

```
/* Inherit parent's border */
p { border: inherit; }
```

Inheritance enables you to apply a style to a common ancestor whenever you find a place in which every descendant element needs that same style. This process is more convenient and maintainable than applying the style to every descendant element that needs a specific style. For example, if the text for an entire document needs to be set to a particular color, you can apply the style to the <body> element, which is the common ancestor for all visible elements.

```
/* Set document text color to gray */
body { color: gray; }
```

Now that you have an understanding of the HTML hierarchy and the inheritance concept, the relationship selectors of CSS can be discussed.

Adjacent Selector

The adjacent sibling selector selects the second element if it comes directly after the first element.

```
div+p { color: red; }
```

This selector matches paragraphs that follow <div> elements.

```
<div>Not red</div>
<p>Red</p>
<p>Not red</p>
```

Descendent Selector

The descendent selector matches an element if it is the child or grandchild of another element. It is useful when you want to apply a style to an element only when it resides within another element.

```
div p { background: gray; }
```

The preceding rule applies to the following paragraph because it descends from a `<div>` element:

```
<div>
  <p>Gray</p>
</div>
```

Direct Child Selector

The direct child selector matches its second element if it is the immediate descendant of its first element.

```
div > span { color: green; }
```

When applied to the following markup, this rule will color the second `<span>` element green. The first `<span>` element is not colored because it is not a direct child of `<div>`.

```
<div>
  <p>
    <span>Not green</span>
  </p>
  <span>Green</span>
</div>
```

General Sibling Selector

CSS 3 added the general sibling selector, which matches the second element only if it is preceded by a sibling element of the first type.

```
h1~p { color: blue; }
```

In the following example, the last two paragraphs are selected because they are preceded by <h1> and all share the same parent:

```
<p>Not blue</p>
<h1>Not blue</h1>
<p>Blue</p>
<p>Blue</p>
```

The general sibling selector is supported by all major browsers, including Chrome 1+, Firefox 3.5+, Safari 3.2+, Opera 10+, and IE 7+.

CHAPTER 7

Specificity

When more than one rule applies to the same element and they specify the same property, there is a priority scheme that determines which rule is given precedence. In short, CSS gives priority to the rule that has the most specific selector.

Selector Specificity

There are some basic rules for calculating specificity. The lowest specificity with the weight of 0 is given by the universal selector (*), which matches all elements in the document.

```
* { color: red; } /* 0 */
```

Type selectors and pseudo-elements have the weight of 1, so a selector containing two type selectors and a pseudo-element has a specificity of 3.

```
p { color: blue; } /* 1 */
body p::first-letter { color: gold; } /* 3 */
```

Class selectors have a weight of 10, as do pseudo classes and attribute selectors. Including one of these selectors with a type selector gives a total weight of 11.

```
.a { color: lime; } /* 10 */
p:first-child { color: navy; } /* 11 */
p[class=a] { color: teal; } /* 11 */
```

© Mikael Olsson 2019

M. Olsson, *CSS3 Quick Syntax Reference*, https://doi.org/10.1007/978-1-4842-4903-1_7

Id selectors have a weight of 100, so an id rule overrides most other conflicting styles.

```
#i { color: aqua; } /* 100 */
```

Inline styles have even greater specificity. With a weight of 1000, inline styles outweigh even id rules.

```
<p style="color: black;">Text</p>
```

To override all other conflicting styles, including those defined as inline styles, a declaration can be declared as !important. Note that the !important modifier is applied to individual declarations, not entire rules.

```
p { color: red !important; }
```

If the specificity between two conflicting rules is the same, the cascade is what determines which rule is applied.

Cascade

In CSS, more than one style sheet can influence a document's presentation. This feature is known as cascading (the "C" part of CSS) because the browser merges all style sheets to resolve any conflicts before the styles are applied.

Web documents can have style sheets that come from three different sources: the browser, site designer and user reading the document. The designer's style sheet usually has the highest priority, followed by the user's personal style sheet (if any) and then the browser's default one.

Designer Styles

As discussed earlier, web designers have three ways to include CSS rules: inline styles, internal style sheets, and external style sheets. Among these three, inline styles are given the highest precedence, followed by internal style sheets and then external style sheets.

If the web page includes more than one external style sheet with conflicting rules (same specificity), the style sheet that is included last in the HTML markup is given precedence. This is also true within a style sheet. If the selectors are the same, the property declared last is the one that counts.

```
p { color: orange; } /* overridden */
p { color: silver; } /* dominant */
```

For inherited styles, an element's own style has priority over style inherited from its ancestors.

```
p { color: orange; } /* dominant */
body { color: silver; }
```

Specificity Guidelines

As shown in this chapter, the style of an element can be specified in many different places and with different priorities. The cascading feature gives a lot of flexibility to CSS, but it can also result in unnecessary complexity if not managed well.

In general, you want to keep specificity low to make it easier to know which rules will take precedence. This way, you can allow the cascade to work for you by adjusting the order in which your style rules appear, instead of needlessly increasing the specificity with id and !important to override conflicting styles.

41

CHAPTER 8

Colors

There are several different ways to specify a color in CSS, which are described in the following sections.

Named Notation

Colors can be set by simply typing the common name of that color.

```
p { color: red; } /* color paragraphs red */
```

The HTML and CSS color specification includes 140 predefined color names, such as white, lime, and olive. These colors are all supported by the major browsers.

Hexadecimal Notation

For the full palette, the red, green, and blue components of the color can be set individually. Each color component consists of a two-digit hexadecimal number, and the whole six-digit number is prefixed by a hash sign (#RRGGBB). Hexadecimal means base-16 counting, so valid digits are 0 through 9 and A through F. Each red-green-blue pair can range from 00 to FF, or 0-255 in decimal notation. All in all, this provides 16 million colors to choose from.

```
p { color: #FF0000; } /* red:255, green:0, blue:0 */
```

© Mikael Olsson 2019
M. Olsson, *CSS3 Quick Syntax Reference*, https://doi.org/10.1007/978-1-4842-4903-1_8

Although this color notation is the most obfuscated one, it is also the most common one because of its precision, conciseness, and browser support. An easy way to discover the hexadecimal value of a color is to use a color picker tool, for instance the one provided by the Google search engine when searching for "color picker."

Short Hexadecimal Notation

There is a short form of the hexadecimal notation in which the color is specified using only three hexadecimal digits instead of six. This notation can be converted to the hexadecimal notation by duplicating each digit.

```
p { color: #f00; } /* same as #ff0000 */
```

The short hexadecimal notation is a useful shortcut when the full precision provided by the longer hexadecimal notation is not needed.

RGB Notation

The rgb() function allows a color value to be specified as three intensity values for the color components red, green, and blue. The value can be either an integer between 0 and 255 or a percentage.

```
p { color: rgb(255, 0, 0); }
p { color: rgb(100%, 0%, 0%); }
```

This notation allows the same color precision as the hexadecimal notation. What notation to use comes down to a matter of preference, but the hexadecimal notation is often preferred because it is shorter and can easily be copied from an image editor, for example.

RGBA Notation

CSS 3 introduced the RGBA notation, adding an alpha value for specifying the color transparency. This alpha value is a number between 0.0 (fully transparent) and 1.0 (fully opaque).

```
/* Red with 50% transparency */
p { color: rgba(100%, 0%, 0%, 0.5); }
```

RGBA color values are supported in Chrome 1+, Firefox 3+, Safari 3.1+, Opera 10+, and IE 9+. If support is not present, the rule is ignored, so if legacy browser support is required a fallback color value can be set as shown here:

```
p {
  color: rgb(100%, 0%, 0%); /* fallback */
  color: rgba(100%, 0%, 0%, 0.5);
}
```

A browser that does not support RGBA ignores the second declaration and continues to apply the opaque version.

HSL Notation

A color value can be set with the hsl() function (which stands for hue, saturation, and lightness). Hue is a degree on a color circle from 0 to 360, where 0 and 360 are red, 120 is green, and 240 is blue. Saturation is a percentage value, with 0% giving a shade of gray and 100% giving the full color. Lightness is also specified as a percentage, from 0% (dark) to 100% (bright).

```
p { color: hsl(0, 100%, 100%); }
```

45

HSL colors are arguably more intuitive to adjust compared with RGB colors, but keep in mind that legacy browsers such as IE 8 do not support them. HSL is a CSS 3 value and is supported in Chrome 1+, Firefox 1+, Safari 3.1+, Opera 10+, and IE 9+.

HSLA Notation

Similar to RGB, the HSL notation can be extended with an alpha value for specifying the transparency.

```
/* Red with 50% transparency */
p { color: hsla(0, 100%, 100%, 0.5); }
```

HSLA is supported in Chrome 1+, Firefox 3+, Safari 3.1+, Opera 10+, and IE 9+, same as the RGBA function.

CHAPTER 9

Units

There are several units to choose from when specifying the size of a property's value.

Absolute Units

The absolute units of length are centimeter (cm), millimeter (mm), and inch (in). Although these units are meant to look the same regardless of the screen resolution, it is not always the case because web browsers do not always know the exact physical size of the display medium.

```
.one-cm { font-size: 1cm; }
.one-mm { font-size: 1mm; }
.one-in { font-size: 1in; }
```

These units are mainly useful when the size of the output medium is known, such as for content that will be printed to paper. They are not recommended for screen displays since screen sizes can vary a lot.

Typographical Units

Points (pt) and picas (pc) are typographical units. By definition, there are 72 points to an inch and 12 points to one pica. Like the absolute units, the typographical units are most useful for print style sheets, not for onscreen use.

© Mikael Olsson 2019
M. Olsson, *CSS3 Quick Syntax Reference*, https://doi.org/10.1007/978-1-4842-4903-1_9

```
.one-point { font-size: 1pt; }
.one-pica  { font-size: 1pc; }
```

Relative Units

The relative units of length are pixel (px) and percentage (%). A percentage is a unit proportional to the parent's value for that property; a pixel is relative to the physical pixel on the display device used.

```
.one-pixel   { font-size: 1px; }
.one-percent { font-size: 1%; }
```

Pixels and percentages are two of the most useful units in CSS for onscreen displays. Pixels are fixed size, so they allow very precise control over the layout in a web document. Percentages, on the other hand, are useful for defining font sizes for text content because the text remains scalable, which is important for small devices and accessibility purposes. When the text is part of the design and needs to match other elements, it can be sized in pixels for greater control. Modern browsers all support full-page zooming, which has made pixel-based font sizes more acceptable. Note that for high-resolution screens, a CSS pixel renders as multiple screen pixels. For example, the first Apple Retina display renders all pixel dimensions as four physical pixels.

Font-Relative Units

Two additional relative measures are em-height (em) and ex-height (ex). Em-height is the same as the font-size; ex-height is about half the font-size.

```
.one-ex { font-size: 1ex; }
.one-em { font-size: 1em; }
```

Like percentage, em-height is a good relative unit that is commonly used for setting the font size of web document text. They both respect the user's choice of font size in their browser and are easier to read on small-screen devices than pixel-based font sizes. The ex-height unit on the other hand is not commonly used.

CSS 3 introduced two additional font-relative units: rem and ch. The root em-height (rem) unit is relative to the font-size of the root element (<html>), which by default is 16px in most browsers. It can be used instead of em to prevent the element's font size from being affected by changes to the font size of its ancestor elements.

```
html { font-size: 16px; }
.one-rem { font-size: 1rem; }
```

The character unit (ch) measures the width of the character zero (0) for the element's font. It can be useful for defining the width of a box containing text because the unit roughly corresponds to the number of characters that fit within that box.

```
/* Same width */
<div style="width: 5ch;"></div>
<div>00000</div>
```

The ch unit is supported as of Chrome 27+, Firefox 19+, Safari 7+, Opera 15+, and IE 9+, so it should be used only together with a fallback. The rem unit has slightly better support and works in Chrome 4+, Firefox 3.6+, IE 9+, Safari 4.1+, and Opera 11.6+.

Viewport Units

Viewport width (vw) and viewport height (vh) units allow elements to be dimensioned relative to the viewport, meaning the visible portion of the document. Each unit represents a percentage of the current viewport.

```
width:  50vw; /* 50% of viewport width */
height: 25vh; /* 25% of viewport height */
```

Two additional viewport units are `vmin` and `vmax`, which give the minimum or maximum value of the viewport's dimension.

```
width:  1vmin; /* 1vh or 1vw, whichever is smallest */
height: 1vmax; /* 1vh or 1vw, whichever is largest */
```

Chrome 26+, Firefox 19+, Safari 6.1+, Opera 15+, and Edge 16+ support all the viewport units. The `vh`, `vw`, and `vmin` units have greater support than `vmax`, going back to Chrome 20+, Safari 6, and IE 10+.

Unit Values

It is possible to set length using decimals. Some properties also allow negative values for length.

```
p { font-size: 0.394in; } /* decimal value */
p { margin: -1px; } /* negative value */
```

Note that a rule does not work if there is a space before the unit or if no unit is specified—except for the value zero. Including a unit after zero is optional, but it is good practice to omit it.

```
p { font-size: 1ex; }   /* correct */
p { font-size: 0; }     /* correct */
p { font-size: 0ex; }   /* correct */
p { font-size: 1 ex; } /* invalid */
p { font-size: 1; }     /* invalid */
```

Whenever a CSS declaration contains an error, it is ignored by the browser. Any other valid declarations in the rule still apply.

Variables

CSS 3 added support for variables to allow for an easy way to store a named value in a single location that can be reused throughout the style sheet. Variable names start with two dashes (--) and are case sensitive. They can be specified inside a selector to limit their scope or inside the html selector to allow them to be referenced from any selector within the style sheet.

```
html { --bg-color: black; }
```

The var function is used to insert the variable's value, which in this example applies a black background to elements that use this content class. An added benefit of variables is that they provide a more human readable format for the value, to convey its intended use.

```
.content { background-color: var(--bg-color); }
```

A second parameter can be passed to the var function. This value will be used if the variable is unavailable, for instance if it hasn't yet been defined.

```
.content {
  width: var(--content-width, 80%);
}
```

Variables are supported by Chrome 49+, Firefox 31+, Safari 1+, Opera 36+, and Edge 15+. Note that IE does not support variables. If legacy browser support is needed another way to achieve the benefits of variables, along with other programming functionalities, is to use a CSS preprocessor such as SASS.[1] However, this adds a layer of complexity since the SASS code will need to be compiled into CSS to be used.

---

[1]https://sass-lang.com

Calculations

The calc function allows property values to be calculated using simple expressions. It can be called anywhere a number is allowed and may include any of the four arithmetic operators (+, -, /, and *). Different units can be used for different parts of the expression, as seen here.

```
.content { width: calc(50% - 1em); }
```

It is possible to combine calc with variables, as seen in the following example where the resulting width is 25px.

```
.content {
  --widthA: 50px;
  --widthB: calc(var(--widthA) / 2);
  width: var(--widthB);
}
```

Browsers supporting the calc function include Chrome 26+, Firefox 16+, Safari 7+, Opera 15+, and IE 9+.

CHAPTER 10

CSS Properties

Now that the basics of CSS have been covered it is time to look at the multitude of properties that are available. In the following chapters, possible property values will be given using a formal notation, such as the one shown here:

```
text-shadow : inherit | none | <offset-x> <offset-y>
              [<blur-radius>] [<color>]
```

This notation means that the `text-shadow` property can have one of three different kinds of values. The default value is listed first; in this case, it is `inherit`. Because the `inherit` keyword can be set for any property, it will not be included in the list unless it is the default value. The second value, `none`, is also a keyword. It is the initial value for this property and can be applied to disable an inherited property effect.

The third option in this notation includes a set of four values—two required ones and two optional ones—as indicated by the square brackets ([ ]). The angle brackets (<>) show that they are not keywords; they are other value types. In this case, they are three length values and a color value. Following this notation, the following declaration shows a valid example use of the `text-shadow` property:

```
text-shadow: 1px 1px 1px red;
```

© Mikael Olsson 2019
M. Olsson, *CSS3 Quick Syntax Reference*, https://doi.org/10.1007/978-1-4842-4903-1_10

Generic Keywords

In addition to `inherit`, there are two other generic property keywords you might come across in CSS: `initial` and `unset`. Both generic keywords were introduced in CSS 3 and can be set on any properties.

The `initial` keyword applies a property's initial value to an element, as defined by the CSS specification. It is supported in Chrome 4+, Firefox 19+, Safari 3.2+, Opera 15+, and Edge 12+. IE 6-11 has no support for this keyword, but Microsoft's Edge browser started out with support for it. Keep in mind that Edge started out with version 12 superseding IE 11, so a CSS feature supported in IE is also supported in Edge. Until IE usage drops sufficiently low the usefulness of the `initial` keyword is limited. It is recommended to instead explicitly specify the initial value for a given property to reset it.

The third generic keyword is `unset`, which is a combination of the `initial` and `inherit` keywords. It resets the property to its inherited value, if there is one; otherwise, it sets the property to the initial value. Support for the `unset` keyword is limited to Chrome 41+, Firefox 27+, Safari 9.1+, Opera 28+, and Edge 13+. No version of IE supports this keyword.

Quirks Mode

When HTML and CSS became standardized by the World Wide Web Consortium (W3C), web browsers could not just comply with the standards because doing so would break most web sites already in existence. Browsers instead created two separate rendering modes: one for new standard compliant sites (full standards mode) and one for old legacy sites (quirks mode).

In full standards mode, the browser does its best to render the page in accordance with HTML and CSS specifications, which is what you want when designing a website. In contrast, quirks mode accounts for bugs in legacy browsers (particularly IE 4 & IE 5) to make old web pages display as their authors intended. Browsers use the doctype for the sole purpose of deciding between full standards mode and quirks mode. A valid doctype at the start of a web document, such as the HTML 5 doctype seen following, ensures that the page is rendered in full standards mode:

```
<!DOCTYPE html>
<html> ... </html>
```

This doctype triggers full standards mode in all major browsers, dating back as far as IE 6.

Vendor Prefixes

Many browsers begin incorporating new CSS properties long before their specification becomes stable. Because these implementations are experimental, their property names include a vendor prefix to indicate that the specification could potentially change in the future.

The major vendor prefixes include -moz for Firefox; -ms for Internet Explorer and Edge; -o for Opera prior to version 15; and -webkit for Chrome, Safari, Android, and iOS. As of version 15.0 Opera also started using the WebKit rendering engine and therefore added support for the -webkit prefix in parallel with the -o prefix. For example, support for the CSS 3 border-radius property can be increased by using the following vendor prefixes. Note that the unprefixed version should always be included last.

```
.round {
  /* Safari 3-4, iOS 1-3.2, Android 1.6-2.0 */
  -webkit-border-radius: 3px;

  /* Firefox 1-3.6 */
  -moz-border-radius: 3px;
```

```
  /* Opera 10.5+, IE 9+, Safari 5+, Chrome 1+,
     Firefox 4+, iOS 4+, Android 2.1+ */
  border-radius: 3px;
}
```

As time goes on, the new property's specification becomes stable, and browsers drop the vendor prefix. Given more time, web users abandon old browsers in favor of new versions, and the need for vendor prefixes diminishes. This has already occurred for the border-radius property, and developers are now encouraged to drop the prefixes, making things a little easier for web developers worldwide.

Progressive Enhancement

When deciding whether to use a recent CSS feature, it is important to consider how your site will look without it. If the feature enhances the appearance of your site, such as the CSS 3 border-radius property, you might want to start using the feature, even when it is viewable by only a small percentage of your visitors. Time works in your favor, and as people abandon old browsers, a greater number of your visitors can see the feature, which enhances their experience on your site. This is the essence of progressive enhancement.

On the other hand, if your site depends on the feature and appears broken without it, you need to carefully consider how well supported the feature is and whether there are fallbacks or scripts you can make use of to increase this support. There are often many ways to achieve the same result in CSS, so it is a good idea to choose a method that is well supported by all major browsers for the key elements of your site, such as the layout.

CHAPTER 11

Text

The text properties serve to format the visual appearance of text content.

color

The `color` property sets the color of text by using either one of the color notations. By default, its value is set to `inherit`, meaning that it inherits the color of its parent element.

```
color : inherit | <color>
```

The initial value is black for all major browsers. In the following example rule, paragraphs are colored blue:

```
p { color: #00f; }
```

text-transform

`text-transform` controls text casing. Possible values are listed as follows, with none as the initial value:

```
text-transform : inherit | none | uppercase | lowercase |
capitalize
```

© Mikael Olsson 2019
M. Olsson, *CSS3 Quick Syntax Reference*, https://doi.org/10.1007/978-1-4842-4903-1_11

This property enables text to be converted into either uppercase or lowercase letters. The `capitalize` value capitalizes the first letter of each word. This property inherits by default, so the none value can be used to remove an inherited `text-transform` effect.

```
text-transform: none; /* remove effect */
```

text-decoration

One or more visual effects to text can be added with the `text-decoration` property.

```
text-decoration : none | underline + overline + line-through + blink
```

To add multiple decorations, separate the values with spaces (indicated by the "+" sign, shown previously). The following rule adds a line above and below text content that is affected by this class:

```
.highlight { text-decoration: underline overline; }
```

This property does not inherit, but its effect renders across descendent inline elements in a way that is similar to inheritance.

text-indent

The first line of text in a block element can be indented with the `text-indent` property. It can be set to a unit of measure or a percentage of the parent element's width. Text can also be indented backward by using a negative value.

```
text-indent (block) : inherit | <length> | <percentage>
```

Note that this property can only be set for block elements, such as the paragraph element <p>. The following example indents the first line of paragraph elements by one em:

```
p { text-indent: 1em; }
```

text-align

The text content of a block element can be aligned with the text-align property. This property can replace usages of the deprecated align attribute in HTML.

```
text-align (block) : inherit | left | center | right | justify
```

Text and inline elements can be aligned to the left, aligned to the right, or centered. The justify value also stretches each line so that both the right and left margins appear straight.

```
p { text-align: justify; }
```

The text-align property inherits, so it needs to be explicitly changed in child elements to restore default left alignment.

direction

The writing direction of text can be switched with the direction property.

```
direction (block) : inherit | ltr | rtl
```

The default value is ltr, meaning left-to-right. It can be changed to rtl to make text content within a block element flow to the right. It indicates that the text is supposed to be read from right-to-left, as in Hebrew or Arabic text, for example.

```
<p style="direction: rtl">
  Aligned from right-to-left
</p>
```

This property does inherit, so it can be set once for the `<body>` element to apply to the whole web page.

text-shadow

A shadow effect can be added to text with the `text-shadow` property.

`text-shadow : inherit | none | <offset-x> <offset-y> [<blur-radius>] [<color>]`

The shadow is defined using two offset values, followed by two optional values for the blur radius and color. The x and y offsets are specified as length values relative to the text. Positive values move the shadow right and down; negative values move it left and up.

A blur effect can be added by setting a blur radius, which makes the shadow stretch and fade at the edges. The final optional value for the property is the color of the shadow. If no color value is specified, most browsers render the shadow in the same color as the text. The following example style causes a slightly blurred gray shadow to appear at the top right of `<h1>` elements:

`h1 { text-shadow: 1px -1px 1px gray; }`

`text-shadow` is a CSS 3 property that is supported by most major browsers, including Chrome 2+, Firefox 3.5+, Safari 1.2+, Opera 9.5+, and, IE 10+.

box-shadow

In addition to text, a shadow effect can be added to block elements with the box-shadow property.

```
box-shadow (block) : inherit | none | [inset] <offset-x>
<offset-y> [<blur-radius>] [<spread-radius>] [<color>]
```

The values for the box shadow are the same as for text-shadow—with two exceptions. A fourth length value, spread-radius, can be specified to grow or shrink the shadow. This value is optional and is 0 if left unspecified, rendering the shadow in the same size as the element. As an example, the following class rule displays a blurry gray shadow to the bottom right of any block element using this class:

```
.drop-shadow { box-shadow: 3px 3px 3px 6px #ccc; }
```

The second value unique to the box-shadow property is the inset keyword. If present, the shadow displays inside the box instead of as a drop shadow on the outside.

```
.inset-shadow { box-shadow: inset 3px 3px 3px 6px #ccc; }
```

box-shadow is a CSS 3 property and is implemented in Chrome 10+, Firefox 4+, Safari 5.1+, Opera 10.5+, and, IE 9+. Support can be expanded using the -webkit and -moz prefixes, as shown here:

```
.drop-shadow
{
  /* Chrome 1-5, Safari 2-5.1+ */
  -webkit-box-shadow: 3px 3px 5px 6px #ccc;

  /* Firefox 3.5-3.6 */
  -moz-box-shadow: 3px 3px 5px 6px #ccc;

  box-shadow: 3px 3px 5px 6px #ccc;
}
```

text-rendering

By default, browsers will automatically decide whether to optimize for speed, legibility or geometric precision when rendering text. This behavior can be changed using the text-rendering property.

```
text-rendering (text elements) : inherit | auto | optimizeSpeed |
optimizeLegibility | geometricPrecision
```

Optimizing for legibility is often desirable, but keep in mind this can have a negative impact on performance, particularly when applied to text heavy pages and viewed on mobile devices.

```
p.legibility {
  text-rendering: optimizeLegibility;
}
p.speed {
  text-rendering: optimizeSpeed;
}
```

The text-rendering property is not defined by any CSS standard but is supported by WebKit and Gecko browsers, including Chrome 4+, Firefox 3+, Safari 5+, and Opera 15+.

CHAPTER 12

Text Spacing

The following properties deal with the space between text content. They are all inherited by default.

line-height

`line-height` sets the distance between lines. The initial value is `normal`, which is typically rendered as 120% of the font size. The line height can also be set to a length, a percentage of the current font size, or a dimensionless number that is multiplied with the current font size.

```
line-height : inherit | normal | <length> | <percentage> |
<number>
```

The `line-height` property inherits, so the preferred way to set `line-height` is by using a dimensionless number. Setting `line-height` as a length or percentage can have unexpected results for child elements that use different font sizes because the inherited line height is then fixed instead of relative to the child element's font size.

```
/* Line height is 1.5 times font size */
line-height: 1.5;
```

Line height has no effect on replaced inline elements such as `<img>`. When used on other (nonreplaced) inline elements, it sets the line height as expected. For block elements, `line-height` sets the minimal height of line boxes within the element.

© Mikael Olsson 2019
M. Olsson, *CSS3 Quick Syntax Reference*, https://doi.org/10.1007/978-1-4842-4903-1_12

word-spacing and letter-spacing

word-spacing sets the spacing between words, and letter-spacing sets the spacing between individual characters. Negative values are allowed for both of these properties.

```
word-spacing : inherit | normal | <length>
letter-spacing : inherit | normal | <length>
```

The following rule creates a 3-pixel distance between letters and a 5-pixel distance between words inside of paragraphs:

```
p {
  letter-spacing: 3px;
  word-spacing: 5px;
}
```

white-space

The white-space property changes the way whitespace characters inside of a block element are handled.

```
white-space (block) : inherit | normal | nowrap | pre | pre-
wrap | pre-line
```

Multiple whitespace characters are normally collapsed into a single character in HTML, and text is wrapped as necessary to fill the width of the containing block element.

```
/* Wrap text and collapse newlines, spaces and tabs */
p { white-space: normal; }
```

Setting whitespace to `nowrap` prevents text from wrapping for anything other than the line break tag `<br>`. The `pre` (preformatted) value also prevents wrapping, as well as preserving all whitespace characters. Its behavior is the same as the `<pre>` element in HTML.

Both the `pre-wrap` and `pre-line` values allow text to wrap as normal, with `pre-wrap` preserving sequences of whitespace and `pre-line` collapsing them. The difference between `pre-line` and `normal` is that `pre-line` preserves newline characters.

CHAPTER 13

Font

The font properties can be used to change aspects of the font and to load custom fonts. They can be applied to any element and they all inherit.

font-family

font-family sets the face of the font. Its value can be a specific font name such as times or verdana; or a generic family name such as sans-serif, serif, or monospace.

```
font-family : inherit | <family-names> | <generic-families>
```

The value for this property is a prioritized list of one or more font names. If a browser does not have access to the first font, it uses the next font and so on.

```
font-family: "Times New Roman", times, serif;
```

It is recommended to end the list with a family name to make sure that at least the font family is consistent across browsers. Note that if a font name includes spaces, it must be surrounded by double quotes, as in the previous example.

© Mikael Olsson 2019
M. Olsson, *CSS3 Quick Syntax Reference*, https://doi.org/10.1007/978-1-4842-4903-1_13

font-size

font-size sets the size of the font. The value can be any unit of measure or a percentage of the parent's font size. There are also a couple of predefined values, as listed here:

```
font-size : inherit | <length> | <percentage> |
            smaller | larger | xx-small | x-small |
            small | medium | large | x-large | xx-large
```

The larger and smaller values are relative to the parent's font size; the other predefined values refer to absolute sizes. The initial size is medium, which is 1 em (16 pixels) for normal text.

font-style

font-style makes the text slanted. According to specifications, italic is a cursive companion face to the normal face, and oblique is a slanted form of the normal face. Both faces tend to be rendered the same way for most fonts, however.

```
font-style : inherit | normal | italic | oblique
```

font-variant

font-variant can be used to display text using small caps instead of lowercase letters. A value of small-caps renders text in uppercase letters that are smaller than regular uppercase letters.

```
font-variant : inherit | normal | small-caps
```

font-weight

font-weight sets the thickness of the font. The borer and lighter values set the thickness relative to the parent element, and the numeric values specify absolute weights. The value of bold is equal to 700, and normal is the same as 400.

```
font-weight : inherit | normal | bold | bolder |
              lighter | 100 | 200 | ... | 900
```

Even if several weight values can be specified, most fonts have only one type of bold, as shown in the following example rendering:

lighter normal **bold bolder** 100 200 300 400 500 **600 700 800 900**

font

There is a convenient shorthand property named font that sets all the font properties in one declaration.

```
font : inherit | <font-style> + <font-variant> +
       <font-weight> + <font-size> / <line-height> +
       <font-family>
```

The properties must be specified in the order listed previously. As long as this order is kept, either one of the properties can be left out (except for font-size and font-family, which are mandatory). If a property is left out, the default value for that property is used, which is to inherit the parent's value. The following example applies four font properties to the paragraph element:

```
p { font: italic 50%/125% Verdana; }
```

This font declaration sets the `font-style`, `font-size`, `line-height`, and `font-family` properties in one declaration. Because `font-variant` and `font-weight` are not included, a side effect of using this declaration is that they are both re-set to inherit the parent's value.

Custom Fonts

Selected fonts can be seen only if the font is installed on the device used to view the web site. If a nonstandard font is needed, a `@font-face` rule can be used to load the font from an online location.

```
@font-face {
  font-family: MyFont;
  src: url(myfont.ttf);
}
```

This rule creates a font named `MyFont` and provides a URL from which the browser can download it. With this rule in place, the custom font can be used just like any standard font.

```
p { font-family: "MyFont", arial, sans-serif; }
```

This use of the `@font-face` rule is supported in Chrome 5+, Firefox 3.5+, Safari 3.1+, Opera 10+, and IE 9+. If the browser does not support the custom font, it reverts to the next standard font in the list.

CHAPTER 14

Background

The background properties can add background effects. None of these properties inherits and they can be applied to any elements.

background-color

The color of an element's background is set with the `background-color` property. By default, its value is set to `transparent`.

```
background-color : transparent | <color>
```

Even if a background image is used, it is a good idea to set a background color. That way, there is a fallback color in case the background image is unavailable for any reason.

```
background-color: #ccc;
```

background-image

`background-image` specifies an image to use as a background with the `url` function.

```
background-image : none | url(<url>)
```

© Mikael Olsson 2019
M. Olsson, *CSS3 Quick Syntax Reference*, https://doi.org/10.1007/978-1-4842-4903-1_14

The image location defined with the url function can be either absolute or relative to the location of the CSS file.

```
/* Relative path */
background-image: url(../images/mybg.jpg);
```

```
/* Absolute path */
background-image: url(http://mydomain.com/images/mybg.jpg);
```

background-repeat

By default, the background image repeats itself both horizontally and vertically. This can be changed with the background-repeat property to make the background repeat only horizontally (repeat-x), only vertically (repeat-y), or not at all (no-repeat).

```
background-repeat : repeat | repeat-x | repeat-y | no-repeat
```

background-attachment

When the viewport is scrolled in a browser, a background image normally follows along with the rest of the page. This behavior is determined by the background-attachment property, which has the initial value scroll. If the value is set to fixed, the position of the background is instead relative to the viewport, making the background stay in place even as the page is scrolled.

```
background-attachment : scroll | fixed | local
```

CSS 3 introduced a third value for this property, local, which fixes the background relative to the element's content instead of the whole viewport. With this value, the background scrolls along with the element's content only when that element is scrolled (achieved by using the overflow property). Support for this value was introduced in Chrome 4+, Firefox 25+, Safari 5+, Opera 10.5+, and IE 9+.

background-position

The background-position property is used to position a background image, with one value for vertical placement and another for horizontal. They can both be set to a length or a percentage of the element's size, and negative values are allowed. There are also some predefined values for this property, including top, center, and bottom for vertical placement; and left, center, and right for horizontal placement.

```
background-position : <length> <length> | <percentage>
<percentage> |
                    top/center/bottom + left/center/right
```

By default, a background image is positioned to the top left of its parent element's padding area. Any length values given move the background image relative to these edges. For example, the following property offsets the background 5 pixels down and 10 pixels to the right:

```
background-position: 5px 10px;
```

CSS 3 added a four-value syntax, allowing a choice of which side of the element the image will be positioned relative to. Using this syntax, the background in the next example is positioned relative to the bottom right instead of the top left of the element.

```
background-position: bottom 5px right 5px;
```

This four-value notation is supported only in Chrome 25+, Firefox 13+, Safari 5.28+, Opera 10.5+, and IE 9+.

background-size

The size of a background image is normally the same as the actual size of the image. It can be changed with the background-size property, which allows the background to be resized to a dimension specified in pixels or as a percentage relative to the background positioning area.

background-size (1-2) : auto | <length> | <percentage> | cover | contain

With two values, the first value determines the width of the image and the second value its height.

background-size: 150% 100%;

A single value defines only the width of the image. The height is then implicitly set to auto, preserving the aspect ratio of the image.

background-size: 150%;

The contain and cover keywords size the background to fill the parent container while maintaining the aspect ratio. The cover value ensures that the image completely covers the background positioning area, whereas contain makes sure that the background is contained within the area. Their difference is illustrated in Figure 14-1.

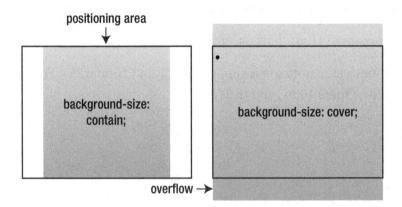

Figure 14-1. *Backgrounds sized with cover and contain keywords*

This property was added in CSS 3 and is supported in Chrome 4+, Firefox 4+, Safari 5+, Opera 10.5+, and IE 9+. Use of the -webkit and -moz prefixes expand support to Chrome 1+, Safari 3+, and Firefox 3.6+.

background-clip

The painting area of a background image or color can be set with the background-clip property.

```
background-clip : border-box | padding-box | content-box
```

The background normally extends to the outside edge of the border (border-box) and renders behind any visible border. A value of padding-box instead draws the background within the element's padding. The third possible value, content-box, draws the background within the content area. Using the following declaration, the background is clipped to the outside edge of the content:

```
background-clip: content-box;
```

background-clip is supported in Chrome 1+, Firefox 4+, Safari 3+, Opera 12+, and IE 9+.

background-origin

The background-origin property determines the starting point of a background image or color.

```
background-origin : padding-box | border-box | content-box
```

A background image is ordinarily rendered starting from the top left of the element's padding area (padding-box). It can be changed so that the background either starts at the top-left edge of the border area (border-box) or the content area (content-box).

The background-origin property is often used together with background-clip to change both the starting point and clipping area of the background. The following declarations set both of them to the content area:

```
background-origin: content-box;
background-clip: content-box;
```

The background-origin property is a CSS 3 property that works in Chrome 4+, Firefox 4+, Opera 10.5+, Safari 5+, and IE 9+. All versions of Firefox and Chrome, along with Safari 4, are supported with the -moz and -webkit prefixes, as seen in the next example. Note that Firefox used the values padding and border prior to version 4; there were no values for specifying the content box as the origin.

```
/* Chrome 1-3, Safari 4 */
-webkit-background-origin: border-box;

/* Firefox 1-3.6 */
-moz-background-origin: border;

background-origin: border-box;
```

background

The background property is a shortcut for setting all background properties in a single declaration.

```
background : <background-color> + <background-image> +
             <background-repeat> + <background-attachment> +
             <background-position> + <background-size> +
             <background-clip> + <background-origin>
```

The order of the values is irrelevant because there is no ambiguity between them. Any one of the values can be left out, but keep in mind that those omitted properties are reset to their defaults when using this property.

```
background: url(bg.png) no-repeat fixed right bottom;
```

In most cases, it is preferable to use shorthand properties such as this one when setting more than one of the individual properties. It has better performance and is easier to maintain than using the equivalent longhand properties seen here:

```
background-image: url(bg.png);
background-repeat: no-repeat;
background-attachment: fixed;
background-position: right bottom;
```

Multiple Backgrounds

More than one background can be applied to the same element by specifying the property values in a comma-separated list. The first background in the list appears at the top, and each successive background is visible only through transparent areas of the backgrounds stacked on top of it.

```
background-image: url(bg1.png), url(bg2.png);
background-repeat: no-repeat, repeat-y;
background-attachment: fixed, fixed;
background-position: right bottom, top left;
```

The shorthand property can also be used with multiple backgrounds in the following way:

```
background: url(bg1.png) no-repeat fixed right bottom,
            url(bg2.png) repeat-y fixed top left;
```

Support for multiple backgrounds was added in CSS 3 and has been included in browsers since Chrome 4+, Firefox 3.6+, Safari 3.1+, Opera 10.5+, and IE 9+. A fallback image can be provided for older browsers that do not support multiple backgrounds.

```
background-image: bg.png; /* fallback */
background-image: bg1.png, bg2.png;
```

CHAPTER 15

Gradients

A gradient is a color fill that blends smoothly from one color to another. Introduced in CSS 3, the gradient functions can be used anywhere an image is required according to specification, but they are mainly used together with the background or background-image properties to create a background gradient.

Linear Gradients

The linear-gradient() function defines a gradient that provides a smooth transition from one color to another.

```
linear-gradient([<angle> | to <side-or-corner>]
              {, <color stop> [stop position]} (2-∞) )
```

In its simplest form, the linear gradient consists of two colors with an even spread from top to bottom. In Figure 15-1, the gradient starts as gray and transitions into black at the bottom.

```
.mygradient {
  background-image: linear-gradient(gray, black);
}
```

© Mikael Olsson 2019
M. Olsson, *CSS3 Quick Syntax Reference*, https://doi.org/10.1007/978-1-4842-4903-1_15

Figure 15-1. *Simple linear gradient*

The angle for the gradient can be set by using the keyword to, followed by the destination in which the gradient will end: top, right, bottom, left, or any combination thereof. An example is shown in Figure 15-2.

```
linear-gradient(to bottom right, gray, black);
```

Figure 15-2. *Bottom-right linear gradient*

More precise angles can be specified by using the deg unit, with 0 deg being the same as to top. The degrees proceed clockwise, and negative angles are allowed.

```
linear-gradient(0deg,    gray, black); /* to top */
linear-gradient(90deg,   gray, black); /* to right */
linear-gradient(180deg, gray, black); /* to bottom */
linear-gradient(-90deg, gray, black); /* to left */
```

Additional color stops can be added between the starting and ending colors. Any color stop can be followed by a stop position specified as either a percentage or a length value. If no stop position is specified, the colors are evenly distributed. In the following case, white is set at 25 percent, instead of its default position of 50 percent. Figure 15-3 illustrates the result of this code.

```
linear-gradient(gray, white 25%, black);
```

Figure 15-3. *Gradient with multiple color stops*

The standard syntax described so far is supported in Chrome 26+, Firefox 16+, Safari 6.1+, Opera 12.1+, and IE 10+. Legacy syntaxes can be used together with the -moz, -webkit, and -o prefixes to expand support down to Firefox 3.6, Chrome 1, Safari 4, and Opera 11.1.

```
.linear-gradient
{
  background-color: red; /* fallback color */

  /* Chrome 1-9, Safari 4-5 */
  background: -webkit-gradient(linear, left top, right top,
  from(red), to(orange));

  /* Chrome 10-25, Safari 5.1-6.1 */
  background: -webkit-linear-gradient(left, red, orange);
```

```
/* Firefox 3.6-15 */
background: -moz-linear-gradient(left, red, orange);

/* Opera 11.1-12.1 */
background: -o-linear-gradient(left, red, orange);

/* Standard syntax */
background: linear-gradient(to right, red, orange);
}
```

Radial Gradients

A radial gradient transitions outward from a central point. In CSS, these gradients are defined with the radial-gradient() function.

```
radial-gradient([<shape> + <size>] [at <position>]
               {, <color stop> [stop position]} {2-∞} )
```

To create a radial gradient, at least two color stops must be defined. The radial gradient in Figure 15-4 starts as gray in the center and fades to black.

```
radial-gradient(gray, black);
```

Figure 15-4. Simple radial gradient

Like linear-gradient(), more than two color stops are allowed and they can optionally be followed by a length or percentage value, indicating the stop position of the color. An example is shown in Figure 15-5.

```
radial-gradient(black 25%, white, black 75%);
```

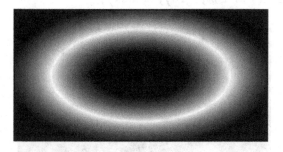

Figure 15-5. *Radial gradient with set stop positions*

The shape of the radial gradient can be either an ellipse or a circle. The default shape is ellipse, which allows the gradient to spread itself to match both the height and width of the element, as shown in Figure 15-5. The alternative circle value, illustrated in Figure 15-6, forces the gradient to be circular, regardless of the shape of the element.

```
radial-gradient(circle, black 25%, white, black 75%);
```

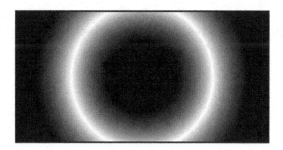

Figure 15-6. *Circular radial gradient*

83

Two length values for the ellipsis or a single value for the circle can be used to set the horizontal and vertical radius of the gradient. For the ellipsis, they can also be percentage values that are relative to the dimensions of the element, as in the example shown in Figure 15-7.

```
radial-gradient(75% 25%, gray, black);
```

Figure 15-7. *Resized radial gradient*

If less precision is needed, the size can be set by using one of the predefined keywords: `closest-side`, `closest-corner`, `farthest-side`, or `farthest-corner`. These values specify whether the gradient is contained by the sides or corners of the element nearest to or farthest away from the origin (see Figure 15-8). For example, the `farthest-side` value sizes the gradient so that its last color ends at the farthest side of the element away from its origin.

```
radial-gradient(farthest-side, gray, black);
```

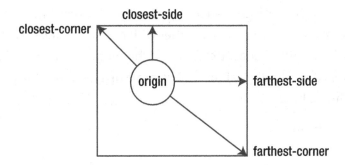

Figure 15-8. *Size keywords*

The origin of a radial gradient is centered by default. It can be changed by specifying the position of the gradient's origin with the keyword at followed by a position specified in the same way as for the background-position property. The horizontal position is specified first, optionally followed by the vertical position. The position can be set with keywords (left, center, right + top, center, and bottom), length values, percentage values, or a combination thereof. An example is given in Figure 15-9, in which the gradient origin is moved to the bottom right of the element.

```
radial-gradient(at right bottom, gray, black);
```

Figure 15-9. *Bottom-right origin*

Support for the radial-gradient() function is largely the same as for linear-gradient() when used together with the -moz, -webkit, and -o vendor prefixes. Like linear-gradient(), the syntax for the radial gradient has gone through some revisions. An example of a full cross-browser syntax is shown here:

```
.radial-gradient
{
  background-color: red; /* fallback color */

  /* Chrome 1-9, Safari 4-5 */
  background: -webkit-gradient(radial, center center, 0px,
  center center, 100%, color-stop(0%,red), color-
  stop(100%,orange));

  /* Chrome 10-25, Safari 5.1-6.1 */
  background: -webkit-radial-gradient(center, ellipse cover,
  red 0%, orange 100%);

  /* Firefox 3.6-16 */
  background: -moz-radial-gradient(center, ellipse cover,
  red 0%, orange 100%);

  /* Opera 11.6-12.1 */
  background: -o-radial-gradient(center, ellipse cover, red 0%,
  orange 100%);

  /* Standard syntax */
  background: radial-gradient(ellipse at center, red 0%,
  orange 100%);
}
```

Repeating Gradients

Linear and radial gradients do not allow gradient patterns to repeat because they naturally stretch to fill the element on which they are defined. Two additional functions are used for creating repeating gradients: `repeating-linear-gradient()` and `repeating-radial-gradient()`.

For the purpose of repeating a linear gradient, the `repeating-linear-gradient()` function is used. The arguments for this function are the same as for `linear-gradient()`.

```
repeating-linear-gradient([<angle> | to <side-or-corner>]
                    {, <color stop> [stop position]} (2-∞) )
```

A repeating linear gradient repeats the color stops infinitely. The size of the gradient is determined by the final color stop. To avoid sharp transitions, the starting color in Figure 15-10 is repeated at the end.

```
repeating-linear-gradient(-45deg, white 0, black 10%, white 20%);
```

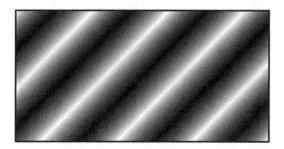

Figure 15-10. *Repeating linear gradient*

The repeating function for the radial gradient also shares the same syntax as the nonrepeating version. The example shown in Figure 15-11 illustrates the repeating function. Note that this gradient has sharp color transitions in contrast with the previous example.

```
repeating-radial-gradient(black, black 5%, white 5%, white 10%);
```

Figure 15-11. *Repeating radial gradient*

The syntax for defining gradients is notably more complex than many other CSS features. For this reason, it can be preferable to use an online tool to graphically design the desired gradient. One such tool can be found on Colorzilla.com.[1] In addition to the standard compliant gradient code, it also provides the prefixed versions necessary for maximum browser compatibility.

---

[1] www.colorzilla.com/gradient-editor

CHAPTER 16

Box Model

The so-called box model of CSS describes the space that is taken up by an HTML element. In this model, each element consists of four boxes: content, padding, border, and margin, as illustrated in Figure 16-1.

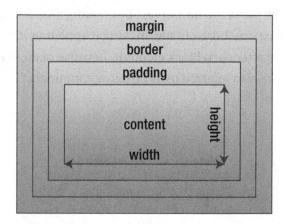

Figure 16-1. *CSS box model*

Each of the three boxes surrounding the content can have different sizes on the top, right, bottom, and left of the element. Any or all of these sizes can also be set to zero.

© Mikael Olsson 2019
M. Olsson, *CSS3 Quick Syntax Reference*, https://doi.org/10.1007/978-1-4842-4903-1_16

Inline and Block

HTML has two primary categories of elements: block and inline. The box model applies differently to these two kinds of elements, so it is important to know the difference between them. Examples of inline elements include <a>, <strong> and <em>, whereas <p>, <h1>, and <form> are block elements.

Inline elements flow along with text content and are split as necessary to fit the width of their container. They may not contain block elements, with the exception of the <a> element, which can wrap any type of element.

Block elements can contain both block and inline elements (see Figure 16-2). They break the flow of text by creating a virtual box around themselves that expand horizontally, making it appear as if there are line breaks before and after each block element. Because of these properties, block elements are also referred to as boxes or containers.

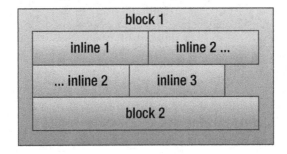

Figure 16-2. *Block and inline elements*

The boxes surrounding inline and block elements have different features. A block element can manipulate all properties in the box model, including the width and height of the content area, as well as the border, padding, and margin. If no width is set, a block element expands horizontally to the maximum allowed by the containing element.

An inline element is more limited in that it cannot set the vertical margins (top or bottom). It also cannot change the width or height of its inline box. For an inline element, the minimum height can be set with the line-height property, but the width and height adjust automatically to fit the content that the element holds.

There is a subcategory of inline elements, called replaced inline elements, that use external objects such as <img>, <video>, and <object>; and form elements such as <input> and <textarea>. With these inline elements, all box properties can be manipulated the same way as block elements.

Span and Div

Using the <span> and <div> elements is a generic way of adding structure to a web document. These elements have no styles associated with them, which makes them especially well suited to work with class and id selectors. The difference between the two is that <span> is an inline element whereas <div> is a block element.

```
<span>Inline</span>
<div>Block</div>
```

As an inline element, <span> is mainly used to add styling to sections of text. It cannot be used for styling block elements because such elements are not allowed inside of inline elements according to the HTML specification.

```
<span style="color: red;">Red text</span>
```

In contrast, <div> is used to create styled containers for other block and inline elements. These custom containers are often what make up the layout of a web page. Because it is a block element, <div> allows all the element's box attributes to be manipulated (width, height, padding, border, and margin).

```
<div class="a">
  <div class="b">Block within a block</div>
</div>
```

Semantic Elements

In HTML 4, the generic <div> element was the main element used for defining sections of a web page to be formatted with CSS. It did not convey any semantic meaning, which was considered a shortcoming of the language. The HTML 5 specification introduced a number of other structural elements you are encouraged to use, such as <header>, <footer>, <section>, <article>, and <nav>.

These new container elements are preferred when they are appropriate given the context, for accessibility and maintainability reasons. Whenever there is not a more semantically suitable element available, the <div> element is still appropriate and continues to be widely used as a generic container. HTML 5 elements became supported in Chrome 6+, Firefox 4+, Safari 5+, Opera 11.5+ and IE 9+.

CSS styling of HTML 5 elements can be added in IE 6-8 with the HTML 5 Shiv script. [1] This JavaScript file can be downloaded and referenced using IE conditional comments, so that it will not affect the performance of modern web browsers:

```
<!--[if lt IE 9]>
  <script src="html5shiv.js"></script>
<![endif]-->
```

---

[1] http://code.google.com/p/html5shiv/

Firefox 3+, Safari 3.1+, and Opera 10+ already allow styling of unknown elements. However, to behave as expected those elements need to be explicitly set to display as block elements since this is not the default styling.

```
header, footer, section, article, aside, details, figcaption,
figure, hgroup, menu, nav {
  display: block;
}
```

CHAPTER 17

Border

The border properties are used to format the border around elements. They can be applied to any element and they do not inherit.

border-style

To make the border visible around an element, the border-style property has to be set to a value other than none, which is the default value.

```
border-style (1-4) | border-top-style |
border-right-style | border-bottom-style |
border-left-style :
  none | dashed | dotted | double | groove |
  hidden | inset | outset | ridge | solid
```

The solid border style is the one most commonly used, but there are several other options for displaying a border, as seen in Figure 17-1. The hidden value removes the border and is synonymous with none, except that it also hides shared borders in tables with collapsed borders.

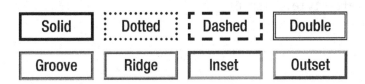

Figure 17-1. *border-style appearances*

© Mikael Olsson 2019
M. Olsson, *CSS3 Quick Syntax Reference*, https://doi.org/10.1007/978-1-4842-4903-1_17

The border-style property is one of several properties that can be set with one to four values. When fewer than four values are specified, the border-style value is duplicated, as shown in Figure 17-2.

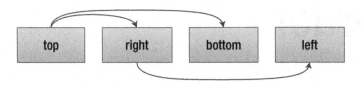

Figure 17-2. *1-to-4-value syntax explained*

Given these rules, the following declarations are synonymous and display a solid border on the top and bottom of an element:

```
border-style: solid none solid none;
border-style: solid none solid;
border-style: solid none;
```

To render all border sides in the same style, only a single style value needs to be specified.

```
border-style: solid;
```

The border-style property has four subproperties that can also be used to target each border side's style.

```
border-top-style:    dotted;
border-right-style:  dashed;
border-bottom-style: ridge;
border-left-style:   inset;
```

border-width

The border-width property, which controls the width of borders, can be set with a unit of length or with one of the predefined values: thin, medium, or thick. The initial value is medium, which is typically rendered as 3 pixels.

```
border-width (1-4) | border-top-width |
border-right-width | border-bottom-width |
border-left-width :
  <length> | thin | medium | thick
```

As with border-style, this property can have one to four values and has four subproperties for setting the individual borders' width.

```
/* Shortcut property */
border-width: thin medium;

/* Full-length properties */
border-top-width:    thin;
border-right-width:  medium;
border-bottom-width: thin;
border-left-width:   medium;
```

A width of zero means that no border is displayed. This value has the same effect as setting the style of the border to none.

border-color

border-color sets the color of the border. CSS does not specify what the default border color should be, but most browsers render it black. This property can have from one to four values and has four subproperties for setting the individual borders' color.

```
border-color (1-4) | border-top-color |
border-right-color | border-bottom-color |
border-left-color :
  <color> | transparent
```

Setting the color to transparent makes the border invisible without changing the layout. As of CSS 3, the transparent keyword may be used anywhere a color value is expected.

```
border-color: transparent;
```

border

The border property can set the width, style and color border properties in a single declaration. It is the most commonly used property for controlling the border.

```
border | border-top | border-right |
border-bottom | border-left :
  <border-width> + <border-style> + <border-color>
```

The values can be set in any order because there is no ambiguity between them. Either one of the values can also be omitted.

```
border: 1px solid black;
```

The border property has four subproperties for specifying the border settings for each of the four sides.

```
border-top:    1px solid red;
border-right:  1px solid blue;
border-bottom: 1px solid aqua;
border-left:   1px solid lime;
```

border-radius

The corners of the border can be rounded using the border-radius property or its four subproperties.

border-radius (1-4) | border-top-left-radius |
border-top-right-radius | border-bottom-right-radius |
border-bottom-left-radius :
  <length> | <percentage> [/ <length> | <percentage>]

The border-radius property can have from one to four values. Each radius value can be set by using either one value for a circle radius or two values for an elliptical radius. The value can be either a length or a percentage. If a percentage is used, it is relative to the container's dimensions. The examples that follow are illustrated in Figure 17-3.

```
.a { border-radius: 5px; }
.b { border-radius: 5px 20px; }
.c { border-radius: 50%; }
.d { border-radius: 30px/10px; }
```

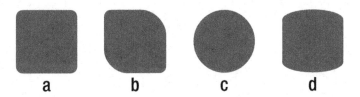

Figure 17-3. Border-radius examples

The radius for each of the four edges can be set using the four subproperties of border-radius. The following example renders the same as the second box in Figure 17-3:

```
border-top-left-radius:     5px;
border-top-right-radius:    20px;
border-bottom-right-radius: 5px;
border-bottom-left-radius:  20px;
```

border-radius is a well-supported CSS 3 property. To add support for older browsers, the -webkit and -moz browser prefixes can be used.

```
.round {
  /* Safari 3-4 */
  -webkit-border-radius: 5px;

  /* Firefox 1-3.6 */
  -moz-border-radius: 5px;

  /* Chrome 1+, Firefox 4+, Safari 5+, Opera 10.5+, IE 9+ */
  border-radius: 5px;
}
```

CHAPTER 18

Outline

The outline is a line drawn around an element, outside the border edge. It is typically rendered as a dotted line around interactive elements to show which element has focus. Although similar to the border, the outline differs in that it does not take up any space in the box model. Furthermore, unlike the border, all four sides of the outline must be the same. The outline properties can be applied to any element, and none of them inherits.

outline-style

The style of the outline is set with the outline-style property. To display the outline, the value needs to be set to something other than none, which is the default.

```
outline-style : none | solid | dotted | dashed | double |
                groove | ridge | inset | outset
```

This property allows the same values as border-style, except that hidden is not a valid outline-style. They are also rendered the same, as illustrated in Figure 18-1.

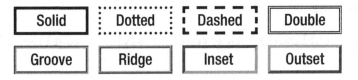

Figure 18-1. *Outline-style appearances*

© Mikael Olsson 2019
M. Olsson, *CSS3 Quick Syntax Reference*, https://doi.org/10.1007/978-1-4842-4903-1_18

outline-width

The thickness of the outline is specified with the outline-width property. Like the border-width property, its value can be a specified length or one of the keywords thin, medium, or thick.

outline-width : <length> | thin | medium | thick

CSS does not define the numerical thickness of these three keywords, but they typically render as 1px, 3px, and 5px, respectively. Like border-width, the initial value for this property is medium.

outline-color

The color of the outline can be changed with the outline-color property. In addition to the standard color notations, the keyword invert is also a valid value for this property.

outline-color : invert | <color>

To ensure proper contrast, the specification suggests that the default value be invert, which sets the outline to the opposite of the color underneath. However, only IE 8+ and Opera 7+ actually support this optional value, so it is not commonly used.

outline

outline is a shorthand property for setting all the preceding outline properties in a single declaration.

outline : <outline-width> + <outline-style> + <outline-color>

The values can be specified in any order because there is no ambiguity between them. Either one of them can be left out.

```
outline: thin solid red;
```

This has the same effect as setting all the individual properties, but with a more convenient syntax:

```
outline-width: thin;
outline-style: solid;
outline-color: red;
```

outline-offset

The space between the outline and the border edge can be set with the outline-offset property introduced in CSS 3.

```
outline-offset : <length>
```

The following declaration moves the outline 3 pixels outward. Negative values are allowed, which instead move the outline inside the element.

```
outline-offset: 3px;
```

Although this property is not supported in IE, it works in all modern browsers, including Chrome 4+, Firefox 2+, Safari 3.1+, Opera 12.1+, and Edge 15+.

CHAPTER 19

Margin and Padding

Margins and padding are used to adjust the position of an element and to create space around it.

Padding

Padding is the space between an element's content and its border. It is set using the padding properties shown here. These properties do not inherit and can be applied to any element.

```
padding (1-4) | padding-top | padding-right |
padding-bottom | padding-left :
  <length> | <percentage>
```

There are four properties for setting the padding on each side individually. In the following example, the vertical (top, bottom) margins will be 10 pixels, and the horizontal (right, left) margins will be zero.

```
padding-top:    10px;
padding-right:  0;
padding-bottom: 10px;
padding-left:   0;
```

These declarations can be shortened to a single declaration using the padding property. The padding values are then specified in clockwise order: top, right, bottom, and left.

```
padding: 10px 0 10px 0;
```

Like many other properties related to the box model, the padding property can be set with one to four values that correspond to the edges of the element's box. With fewer than four values, the padding is repeated as is shown in Figure 19-1.

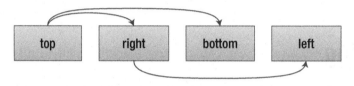

Figure 19-1. *1-to-4-value syntax explained*

For instance, if two values are specified, the first value sets the top and bottom padding, and the second value sets the right and left padding. This gives an even shorter way of writing the previous example.

```
padding: 10px 0;
```

Keep in mind that the padding is part of the element's background and is affected by the background properties, whereas the margin is always transparent.

Margin

The margin is the space around an element's border and is set using the margin properties listed as follows. These properties are not inherited and can be applied to any element, with the exception that vertical margins do not affect nonreplaced inline elements.

```
margin (1-4) | margin-top | margin-right |
margin-bottom | margin-left :
  <length> | <percentage> | auto
```

Margin and padding can both use percentage values, which are relative to the width and height of the containing element. In contrast with padding, margins can be negative, which allows for element areas to overlap. The auto keyword lets the browser automatically calculate the margin.

Like the padding and border properties, the margin property can be set with one to four values. For example, in the following declaration, the top-bottom margins will be 1 cm, and the right-left margins will be 0:

```
margin: 1cm 0;
```

The margin property also has four subproperties, which provide a more verbose method for setting the margin on each of the four sides.

```
margin-top:    1cm;
margin-right:  0;
margin-bottom: 1cm;
margin-left:   0;
```

Top and bottom margins are shared between adjacent boxes, so the vertical distance between two boxes is not the sum of the margins, but only the greater of the two margins. Because of this, the distance between the two following <div> boxes will be only 10 pixels:

```
<div style="margin-bottom: 5px;">Top box</div>
<div style="margin-top: 10px;">Bottom box</div>
```

107

CHAPTER 20

Dimension

The dimension properties control the size of an element, as well as its minimum and maximum dimensions. They do not inherit and can be applied only to block elements and replaced inline elements.

width and height

The width and height of an element's content area can be set with the `width` and `height` properties. These two properties can be assigned with either a length or a percentage value, where the percentage is relative to the parent element's dimensions.

```
width | height : auto | <length> | <percentage>
```

A block element normally stretches out to the edges of its container. In contrast, the element's height collapses to fit its content. With the `width` and `height` properties, these default behaviors can be changed. In the following example, elements applying the class have a width of 100 pixels and a height of 50 pixels. After the dimensions have been set like this, the element keeps that size, no matter how the page is resized.

```
.mybox {
  width: 100px;
  height: 50px;
}
```

min-width and min-height

The min-width and min-height properties set the minimum dimensions of an element. The element's width and height still expand to fit the content, but the element does not collapse below the specified minimum dimensions, which does not include padding, borders, or margins.

min-width | min-height : <length> | <percentage>

Valid values for these properties are lengths and percentages, where percentage is relative to the dimensions of the containing block. For example, the following class makes an element take up at least half of the available width and height:

```
.half {
  min-width: 50%;
  min-height: 50%;
}
```

max-width and max-height

The maximum dimensions of an element's content area are set with the max-width and max-height properties. They can be set with a length or percentage value, as well as the keyword none to clear a previously set value.

max-width | max-height : none | <length> | <percentage>

By setting both the maximum and minimum width, you can define an interval for the way the width of an element can vary. A block element using the following class expands to fill 500 pixels if it can. When horizontal space is limited, the element is allowed to shrink down to no fewer than 200 pixels.

```
.mybox {
  max-width: 500px;
  min-width: 200px;
}
```

The max-width property has priority over min-width. However, it is the other way around with the height properties because min-height has priority over max-height. Thus, an element using the following class has a height of 5 em, unless its content requires more height. In that case, the element expands vertically up to its maximum allowed value of 20 em.

```
.mybox {
  max-height: 20em;
  min-height: 5em;
}
```

Keep in mind that the fixed width and height properties should not be used together with the min- and max- properties. The four min- and max- properties are supported by all major browsers, including Chrome 1+, Firefox 1+, Safari 1+, Opera 8+, and IE 7+. They are popularly used together with media rules for creating fluid layouts that work well across different screen sizes.

box-sizing

The dimension properties normally refer to the content area, not the padding or border area. Therefore, to know the actual width or height that an element occupies in the box model, the surrounding padding and border have to be taken into account.

```
/* 100 pixels wide element */
.mybox {
  padding: 3px;
  border: 2px solid red;
  width: 90px;
}
```

CSS 3 introduced the box-sizing property to allow web developers a choice of how widths and heights are calculated. Its default value is content-box, which means the dimension properties refer only to the content area. The alternative border-box value includes the padding and borders in these measurements.

```
box-sizing : content-box | border-box
```

By changing the box sizing to border-box, you can create a grid layout more easily because you no longer need to take the padding and border sizes into account.

```
/* 100 pixel wide element */
.mybox {
  box-sizing: border-box;
  padding: 3px;
  border: 2px solid red;
  width: 100px;
}
```

The border-box property. does not inherit, but it can be applied to all elements on the website using the universal selector. To increase browser support, the -webkit and -moz prefixes can be used.

```
/* Use border-box for all elements */
* {
  /* Chrome 1-8, Safari 3-5 */
  -webkit-box-sizing: border-box;
```

112

```
/* Firefox 1-28*/
-moz-box-sizing: border-box;

/* Chrome 9+, Firefox 29+, Safari 5.1+, Opera 9.5+, IE 8+ */
box-sizing: border-box;
}
```

Browser support for the box-sizing property has become good enough that all major browsers now support it. As such, many websites employ this property to simplify the grid calculations for their layouts.

CHAPTER 21

Positioning

The positioning properties can change how and where elements are displayed. They enable very precise control over the web page layout.

position

Elements can be positioned in four different ways using the `position` property. An element with the `position` property set to anything but `static` is known as a positioned element.

```
position : static | relative | absolute | fixed
```

A positioned element can be moved with the `top`, `left`, `right`, and `bottom` properties, which can be used to position elements anywhere on the page and also to resize them horizontally and vertically. They allow both positive and negative length and percentage values, with the percentage being relative to the dimensions of the containing block.

```
top | right | bottom | left (positioned) :
  auto | <length> | <percentage>
```

© Mikael Olsson 2019
M. Olsson, *CSS3 Quick Syntax Reference*, https://doi.org/10.1007/978-1-4842-4903-1_21

static

By default, the position property has the value static. This value means that the element appears in its regular position in the page flow and is not affected by the top, left, right, or bottom positioning properties.

```
/* Not positioned element */
.static { position: static; }
```

Because the position property is not inherited, and static is the default, there is no need to explicitly set the position property to static.

relative

Changing the position value to relative means that the element can be positioned relative to its normal position in the page flow. For example, to display a selected element 20 pixels below its normal position, the following declarations are used:

```
/* Move element 20 pixels down */
.relative {
  position: relative;
  top: 20px;
}
```

Relatively positioned elements are considered part of the normal page flow, so other elements do not move to fill in the gap left by the moved element.

The effect of moving an element relative to its normal position can also be achieved by using the element's margin. This solution is often preferable unless there is a specific need to make the element positioned, such as whether it will be a container for an absolutely positioned child element.

```
/* Move element 20 pixels down */
margin-bottom: -20px;
```

Keep in mind that changing the margin affects the layout and fills in gaps, whereas relative positioning does not.

absolute

The position value absolute detaches the element from any containing elements and allows it to be positioned relative to its nearest positioned ancestor or to the document body if there are none.

```
/* Place element in upper left corner */
.absolute {
  position: absolute;
  top: 0;
  left: 0;
}
```

fixed

A fixed element is positioned relative to the screen viewport. It does not move when the page is scrolled. Similar to absolutely positioned elements, fixed elements do not reserve any space in the normal page flow.

```
/* Place element fixed in bottom right corner */
.fixed {
  position: absolute;
  bottom: 0;
  right: 0;
}
```

overflow

The overflow property decides how content overflow is handled for block elements. It defaults to visible, meaning that text and child elements that expand beyond the element's content area are visible. Setting the value to hidden hides the overflowing content, and with the scroll value the element's block becomes scrollable to accommodate the overflowed content. The auto value is similar to scroll, but the scrollbars then appear only when necessary.

```
overflow (block) : visible | hidden | scroll | auto
```

This property controls the behavior of both horizontal and vertical overflow. Two additional properties, overflow-x and overflow-y, can be used to differentiate between how horizontal or vertical overflow is handled. The values for these two properties are the same as for the overflow property.

```
overflow: hidden;    /* hide all overflow */
overflow-x: hidden; /* hide horizontal overflow */
overflow-y: hidden; /* hide vertical overflow */
```

clip

The clip property can crop an element into a rectangle if it is positioned as either absolute or fixed. It uses a CSS function called rect() to specify the clipping region.

```
clip (absolute | fixed) :
  auto | rect(<top>, <right>, <bottom>, <left>)
```

rect() requires four length values, each separated by commas. These values are relative to the top-left corner of the element. The example shown in Figure 21-1 cuts out and displays a 200 x 400 pixel region from the element to which it is applied.

```
.myclip {
  position: absolute;
  clip: rect(100px, 500px, 300px, 100px);
}
```

Figure 21-1. *Shaded region is removed*

The keyword auto can be used as a value for the right or bottom side to refer to the full width or height of the element, respectively. This keyword is also the default value for the clip property, which then means that the element is not clipped.

```
/* Remove 100px from left and top */
clip: rect(100px, auto, auto, 100px);

/* No clipping */
clip: auto;
```

Browser support for the clip property is almost universal: Chrome 1+, Firefox 1+, Safari 1+, Opera 7+, and IE 8+.

z-index

Positioned elements that overlap each other are normally layered according to their order in the web document. This natural stacking order can be altered with the z-index property

```
z-index (positioned) : auto | <integer>
```

The z-index property takes a positive or negative integer as its value, indicating the stacking order. Elements with a higher value are in front of elements with a lower value, as in the following example:

```
<img src="ace-of-hearts.png" style="
  position: absolute;
  left: 0;
  top: 0;
  z-index: 1;">

<img src="ace-of-spades.png" style="
  position: absolute;
  left: 100px;
  top: 100px;
  z-index: 0;">
```

In this example, shown in Figure 21-2, the ace of hearts is layered on top of the ace of spades because of its higher stacking order.

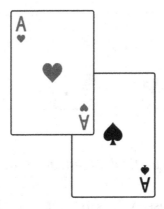

Figure 21-2. *Customized stacking order*

vertical-align

The vertical alignment of text and inline elements within a line can be controlled with the vertical-align property. This property can also be used on table cell elements.

```
vertical-align (inline | table-cell) :
  baseline | <length> | <percentage> | top | middle |
  bottom | text-top | text-bottom | super | sub
```

By default, the bottom of text and inline elements, such as images, align at the baseline, which is the invisible line on which all letters sit. The values top and bottom align the image to the top and bottom of the line, respectively. Less intuitive is the value middle, which aligns the middle of the image with the middle of lowercase letters in the parent. The rendering of these common alignment values is illustrated in Figure 21-3.

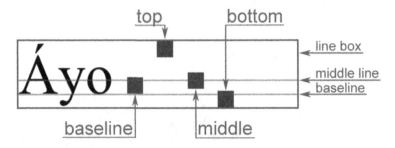

Figure 21-3. Common vertical alignment values

Two less commonly used values for `vertical-align` are `text-bottom` and `text-top`. The `text-bottom` value aligns the bottom of the element with the bottom of the text. Opposite of it, the `text-top` value aligns the top of the element with the top of the text. There is also the `sub` and `super` values, which align the element to subscript and superscript positions, respectively. The result of using these values is shown in Figure 21-4.

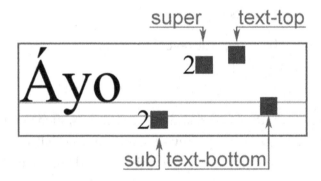

Figure 21-4. Other vertical alignment values

Elements can also be raised (positive value) or lowered (negative value) with either a length or percentage value. Both percentage and length values start at the baseline; the percentage value is relative to the line height.

```
/* Align text segment 5 pixels below normal text */
Normal <span style="vertical-align: -5px;">Lowered</span>
```

When applied to table cell elements <th> and <td>, the `vertical-align` property behaves as the deprecated `valign` attribute in HTML. Valid values for table cells are `baseline`, `bottom`, `middle`, and `top`. Other values, including lengths and percentages, should not be used with table cells.

The `top`. value aligns the cell's top padding edge with the top of the row. Likewise, `bottom` aligns the cell's bottom padding edge with the bottom of the row. More notably, the `baseline` value aligns the cell's content so that it shares the same baseline as other cells that are baseline-aligned.

In contrast with inline elements that default to `baseline`, table cell elements are normally aligned in the middle. For table cells, the `middle` value behaves in a more intuitive way by aligning the cell's padding box in the middle of the row, making the cell's content appear centered.

In the following example, the table cell element is vertically aligned at the bottom:

```
<table>
  <tr>
    <td style="vertical-align: bottom;">Bottom</td>
  </tr>
</table>
```

Centering

There are several ways to center elements in CSS. One method is to use the `text-align` property with the value `center`.

```
.text-center { text-align: center; }
```

By applying this property to a block element, text within it is center-aligned.

```
<p class="text-center">Centered text</p>
```

This method works for text and inline child elements, but not for child block elements. To center block elements, the left and right margins can be set to auto, which makes the horizontal margins equally large, causing the block to be centered.

```
.box-center { margin: 0 auto; }
```

Keep in mind that for a block element to appear centered, its width must be fixed and not flexible; otherwise, it takes up all the available width.

```
<div style="width: 50px; height: 50px;
            border: 1px solid black;"
    class="box-center"></div>
```

For vertical centering, one way to align content to the middle is to use the vertical-align property on the parent element with its value set to middle. This behavior only works as expected for table cell elements, so the container needs to be changed into one, as in the following example using the display property:

```
<div style="vertical-align: middle;
            display: table-cell;
            min-height: 100px;">Centered</div>
```

Simpler control over alignment has been added to CSS with the flexbox module, which will be looked at in a later chapter.

Transformations

The transform property allows for visual manipulation of an element by for instance rotating, skewing, translating, or scaling it.

```
transform (block) : none | rotate(<angle>) | rotateX(<angle>) |
  rotateY(<deg>) | rotateZ(<deg>) | rotate3d(<x>,<y>,<z>,<deg>) |
  skew(<x-deg>[, <y-deg>])> | skewX(<deg>) | skewY(<deg>) |
```

```
translate(<x>,<y>) | translateX(<x>) | translateY(<y>) |
translateZ(<z>) | translate3d(<x>,<y>,<z>) | scale(<x>[, <y>]) |
scaleX(<x>) | scaleY(<y>) | scaleZ(<z>) | scale3d(<x>,<y>,<z>)
matrix(n,n,n,n,n,n)> | matrix3d(n,n,n,n,n,n,n,n,n,n,n,n,n,n,
n,n) |
perspective(<p>)
```

Consider the style rules below that will be used to illustrate how transformations work. Note the float property used here to cause block elements to stack up horizontally instead of vertically.

```
.box {
  float: left;
  width: 100px;
  height: 100px;
  margin: 0 1em;
  background: #ccc;
}

/* Rotate element clockwise 45 degrees */
.a { transform: rotate(45deg); }

/* Tilt element 15 degrees right */
.b { transform: skewX(-15deg); }

/* Move element 25% down and scale height to 50% */
.c { transform: translateY(25%) scaleY(0.5); }
```

The result of applying these styles to a set of block elements can be seen in Figure 21-5.

```
<div class="box a"></div>
<div class="box b"></div>
<div class="box c"></div>
```

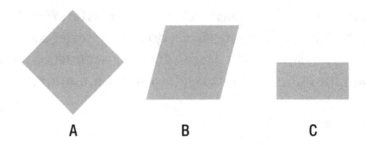

A   **B**   **C**

***Figure 21-5.** Transformed boxes*

The matrix function can perform one or more of the 2d transformations using a set of six values. The first two values are for scaling vertically and horizontally, respectively, with the value 1 meaning no scaling is applied. The second and third values are for skewing the element, and the last two values are for translating the element.

```
/* Scale to half size and skew 45 degrees left and down */
.d { transform: matrix(1,0.5,0,0.5,0,0) }
.e { transform: scaleY(0.5) skew(45deg) }
```

Both of these transformations will produce the same result, which is illustrated in Figure 21-6.

```
<div class="box d"></div>
<div class="box e"></div>
```

D   **E**

***Figure 21-6.** Matrix transformation*

By default the origin of a transformation is the center of the element. This point of origin can be changed using the transform-origin property. The first value is the horizontal position, the second value is the vertical, and the third value represents the position on the Z axis. The third value will only work when using 3d transformations, and it cannot be a percentage.

```
transform-origin (block) : 50% 50% 0 |
  <x-axis: left | center | right | <length> | <%>> +
  <y-axis: top | center | bottom | <length> | <%>> +
  [<z-axis: <length>>]
```

2d transformations, as well as the transform-origin property, are supported in Chrome 4+, Firefox 3.5+, Safari 3.1+, Opera 11.5+ and IE 9+. The 3d transformations were added later and are available as of Chrome 12+, Firefox 10+, Safari 4+, Opera 15+ and IE 10+.

CHAPTER 22

Classification

The classification properties specify how an element is displayed and whether it is visible.

display

The `display` property determines the kind of box that surrounds an element. It can make any element appear as inline, block, or any other type. Every element has a default display value that depends on what type of element it is.

```
display : none | inline | block | list-item | inline-block |
          inline-table | table | table-cell | table-row |
          table-column | table-column-group | table-footer-
          group |
          table-header-group | table-row-group | flex | inline-
          flex |
          grid | inline-grid | run-in
```

Most HTML elements display as either inline or block; others have special display properties, such as `list-item` for the `<li>` element and `table-cell` for the `<td>` and `<th>` elements. By using the `display` property, any element can be changed to be rendered as these or any other element type. For instance, the following link is rendered as a block element instead of an inline element:

```
<a href="#" style="display: block;">Block link</a>
```

One of the more useful values for display is inline-block, which combines features of both block and inline. An inline-block element is like an inline element, except that it can also manipulate the width, height, and vertical margin properties of the box model as a block element does. These features are the same as those of replaced inline elements, such as <img> and <button>. As such, these elements were formally redefined as inline-block elements in HTML 5.

A common application of inline-block is to make list item elements (<li>) suitable for horizontal navigation menus. Note that changing the display type of the list item element from list-item to inline-block automatically removes the list marker.

```
li {
  display: inline-block;
  width: 100px;
  background: #ccc;
}
```

With this rule in place, the following markup renders three boxes with gray backgrounds next to each other, as illustrated in Figure 22-1.

```
<ul>
  <li>Item one</li>
  <li>Item two</li>
  <li>Item three</li>
</ul>
```

| Item one | Item two | Item three |

Figure 22-1. *The inline-block value demonstrated*

Another useful display value is none. It completely hides an element, making the page render as if the element did not exist.

```
.removed { display: none; }
```

visibility

The visibility property can hide an element without removing the space it occupies by setting the property's value to hidden.

```
visibility (block) : inherit | visible | hidden | collapse
```

The collapse value is meant to be used only on certain table elements: rows (<tr>), columns (<col>), column groups (<colgroup>), and row groups (<thead>, <tbody>, and <tfoot>). According to specification, collapse should remove the hidden element (same as display: none) and make the space available for other elements to claim. Regrettably, not all major browsers follow the specification for this value. Setting the display property to none results in more consistent browser behavior and should be used instead.

opacity

The opacity property can make an element and its content transparent.

```
opacity : <number>
```

A decimal value between 0.0 and 1.0 is used to set the transparency. With a value of 1, the element is opaque; 0 renders the element fully transparent, or invisible.

```
.half-transparent { opacity: 0.5;}
```

Support for this CSS 3 property is included in Chrome 1+, Firefox 1+, Safari 1.2+, Opera 9+, and IE 9+. IE support can be enhanced using the following filter:

```
.half-transparent {
  filter: alpha(opacity=50); /* IE 5-8 */
  opacity: 0.5;
}
```

float

The float property detaches an element from its containing element and makes it float on top of it, either to the left or right side. It is intended for wrapping text around images and was also commonly used for making layouts before more modern layout methods became available. Floating an inline element automatically changes it into a block element.

```
float : none | left | right
```

To have text and other inline content wrap around an image, you can float it to the left or right.

```
<img style="float: left;" src="myimage.png" alt="">
```

Floats allow block. elements to be lined up horizontally. For instance, a grid of boxes can be created with the following class:

```
.box {
  float: left;
  width: 100px;
  height: 100px;
  margin: 0 1em;
  background: #ccc;
  border-radius: 10px;
}
```

This class makes boxes stack up horizontally instead of vertically, which is the normal behavior for block elements (see Figure 22-2).

```
<div class="box"></div>
<div class="box"></div>
<div class="box"></div>
```

Figure 22-2. *Floated boxes*

A side effect of using floats. is that any element that follows these floated boxes also lines up horizontally. The clear property is designed to stop this behavior.

clear

The clear property is used to clear floating elements from the left, right, or both sides of an element.

```
clear (block) : none | left | right | both
```

This property is commonly given its own class that has the same name as the property.

```
.clear { clear: both; }
```

An empty div container with the clear class is typically placed after the floated elements. This cleared element is moved below the floating elements instead of appearing next to them.

```
<div class="clear"></div>
```

Because floated layouts tend to be complex and fragile they have largely been superseded by other more modern layout methods, such as the flexbox and grid modules.

cursor

The cursor property specifies what cursor users see when they hover over an element. The default value is auto, meaning that the browser decides what cursor to use. Standard cursor values and their appearance can be seen in Table 22-1.

Table 22-1. *Standard cursor values*

▷	default	🖑	pointer	✥	move		copy
⌛	wait		progress	▷?	help		context-menu
↕	ns-resize	↔	ew-resize	I	text	⊢⊣	vertical-text
↑	n-resize	→	e-resize	↓	s-resize	←	w-resize
↗	ne-resize	↘	se-resize	↙	sw-resize	↖	nw-resize
↙↗	news-resize	↖↘	nwse-resize	✚	cell		alias
⊘	not-allowed	↔‖	col-resize	↕	row-resize	◆	all-scroll
🖑⊘	no-drop	+	crosshair				

In addition to these values, custom cursors can be defined using the url function. If this cursor is not available, a generic cursor can be specified after the custom one, separated by a comma.

```
cursor: url(new.cur), pointer;
```

CHAPTER 23

List

The CSS list properties deal with the list elements, specifically the `<ul>`, `<ol>`, and `<li>` elements.

list-style-type

Lists are rendered with a marker shown before each list item element (`<li>`). The appearance of this marker can be changed using the `list-style-type` property. For an unordered list (`<ul>`), each list item is marked in the same way. The predefined bullet values shown here can be used, with `disc` (a filled circle) as the initial value:

```
list-style-type : inherit | disc | circle | square | none
```

In an ordered list (`<ol>`), each list item is marked with a numeric character to show its position in the sequence. All major browsers support the following numeric types, with `decimal` as the initial value:

```
list-style-type : inherit | decimal | none | upper-alpha |
                  lower-alpha | upper-roman | lower-roman |
                  lower-greek | lower-latin | armenian |
                  georgian | decimal-leading-zero
```

The following example assigns: a new list style for the two list elements. It is possible to make the `<ul>` display ordered markers and the `<ol>` to display unordered markers, but this is not good practice.

© Mikael Olsson 2019
M. Olsson, *CSS3 Quick Syntax Reference*, https://doi.org/10.1007/978-1-4842-4903-1_23

```
ul { list-style-type: square; } /* ■ */
ol { list-style-type: upper-roman; } /* I, II, III, ... */
```

The color of the marker is the same as the text color of the list element. Keep in mind that any element can be made to display list markers by changing its display type to list-item.

list-style-image

As an alternative to the predefined markers, using the list-style-image property allows a custom image to be used as the list bullet.

```
list-style-image : inherit | none | url(<url>)
```

The image path is specified inside of the CSS url function.

```
list-style-image: url(my-bullet.png)
```

This property overshadows any marker type selected with the list-style-type property. Even so, it is a good idea to specify a list-style-type as a fallback in case the custom bullet image is unavailable for any reason.

list-style-position

The list marker is normally positioned outside of the element box. list-style-position provides an alternative: to place the bullet inside of the element box.

```
list-style-position : inherit | outside | inside
```

Selecting outside aligns each line of text with the start of the first line, whereas inside causes successive lines of text to wrap underneath the marker. The inside value also visually indents the marker, as shown in Figure 23-1.

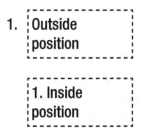

Figure 23-1. *Outside and inside marker placement*

list-style

list-style is the shorthand property for setting all the list properties. The values can be set in any order because there is no ambiguity between them. Any one of the values can also be omitted, in which case the default value for that property is used.

list-style : <list-style-type> + <list-style-image> + <list-style-position>

In the following example, the type and position values of the list-style are set, which are inherited to the list items.

```
<ul style="list-style: inside square;">
  <li>Apple</li>
  <li>Orange</li>
  <li>Pear</li>
</ul>
```

Keep in mind that list properties cannot only style list containers <ul> and <ol>, but also individual list items <li>.

Counters

Elements can be numbered automatically in CSS using the counter-increment and counter-reset properties. The counter-reset property specifies the name of the counter. It is optionally followed by the counter's initial value, which is zero by default.

```
/* Create a counter named chapter */
body { counter-reset: chapter; }
```

The counter-increment property takes the counter's name followed by an optional number. The number, which sets how much the counter is incremented for every occurrence of the element, is 1 by default.

```
/* Increment the counter at each <h1> */
h1:before { counter-increment: chapter; }
```

The final step of creating a counter is to display it by using the CSS counter() function with the name of the counter as its argument. In this example, the chapter number is shown before the <h1> elements:

```
/* Increment and display the counter */
h1:before {
  content: "Chapter " counter(chapter) " - ";
  counter-increment: chapter;
}
```

The counter. now adds the chapter number before <h1> elements.

```
<h1>First</h1>   <!-- Chapter 1 - First -->
<h1>Second</h1>  <!-- Chapter 2 - Second -->
<h1>Third</h1>   <!-- Chapter 3 - Third -->
```

Another counter can be added to also enumerate <h2> subheadings. This counter is here reset to zero at every <h1> element:

```
h2:before {
    content: counter(chapter) "." counter(section) " ";
    counter-increment: section;
}
h1 { counter-reset: section; }
```

The following example illustrates how the counters are displayed:

```
<h1>Head</h1>  <!-- Chapter 1 - Head -->
<h2>Sub</h2>   <!-- 1.1 Sub -->
<h2>Sub</h2>   <!-- 1.2 Sub -->
<h1>Head</h1>  <!-- Chapter 2 - Head -->
<h2>Sub</h2>   <!-- 2.1 Sub -->.
```

Nesting Counters

CSS counters can be nested any number of levels deep. These nested counters can be combined and displayed using a CSS function called counters(). The function's first argument is the counter name, and the second is a string that separates each counter.

```
ul { counter-reset: mycounter; }
li:before {
  content: counters(mycounter, ".") " ";
  counter-increment: mycounter;
}
```

These rules apply to the following unordered lists (note that a new counter instance is automatically created for every nested list):

```
<ul>
  <li>item</li>   <!-- 1 item -->
  <li>item</li>   <!-- 2 item -->
  <ul>
    <li>item</li> <!-- 2.1 item -->
    <li>item</li> <!-- 2.2 item -->
  </ul>
</ul>
```

Counters are supported in all major browsers, including all versions of Chrome, Firefox, Safari, and Opera, as well as IE 8+.

CHAPTER 24

Table

CSS has a number of properties that are used specifically with table elements. These properties offer control over how browsers render tabular data.

border-spacing

The distance between the borders of adjacent table cells can be changed with the border-spacing property, which is the CSS equivalent of the cellspacing attribute in HTML. W3C defines the initial value for this property as 0, but most browsers render it as 2px by default.

```
border-spacing : inherit | <length> [<length>]
```

This property can be specified with either one or two length values. With two values, the first one sets the horizontal spacing, and the second one sets the vertical spacing.

```
.spacing {
  border-spacing: 5px 10px;
}
```

© Mikael Olsson 2019
M. Olsson, *CSS3 Quick Syntax Reference*, https://doi.org/10.1007/978-1-4842-4903-1_24

border-spacing is a property of the table, not the cells, so it is applied to the <table> element as in the following example:

```
<table class="spacing">
  <caption>My Table</caption>
  <tr>
    <td>1st cell, 1st row</td>
    <td>2nd cell, 1st row</td>
  </tr>
  <tr>
    <td>1st cell, 2nd row</td>
    <td>2nd cell, 2nd row</td>
  </tr>
</table>
```

This table. is illustrated in Figure 24-1, with a solid border applied to the <td> elements.

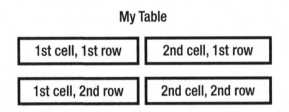

Figure 24-1. *Example table*

Table cells have borders and padding, but they do not have any margins; they have border-spacing instead. Padding works the same as for other elements and behaves like the cellpadding attribute in HTML.

border-collapse

The border-collapse property determines whether the table borders are collapsed into a single border or separated.

border-collapse : inherit | separate | collapse

Normally, table cells have their own distinct borders and are separated by the distance set with the border-spacing property. If the borders are set to collapse instead, the cells share borders, and any value for the border-spacing property is ignored.

table { border-collapse: collapse; }

caption-side

The <caption> element provides a label for a table. Its position can be changed using the caption-side property.

caption-side : inherit | top | bottom

A caption is ordinarily displayed at the top, but it can also be positioned below the table using the caption-side property. This property applies to the <caption> element, but it can also be set for the <table> element since it inherits.

caption { caption-side: bottom; }

empty-cells

A table cell without any content normally still displays its border and background. This behavior can be changed with the empty-cells property.

empty-cells : inherit | show | hide

145

Setting the value for this property to hide causes the cell's border and background to be hidden. The layout of the table is not affected.

table-layout

The table-layout property determines whether the width of table cells should be fixed or flexible. Unlike the other table properties, table-layout is not inherited.

```
table-layout : auto | fixed
```

This property is initially set to auto, which means that the width of table cells automatically expands to fit their content, even if that means going beyond their set width. To enforce a table's specified width, the table-layout can instead be set to fixed. The horizontal layout then depends only on the table's set width, not on the content of the cells.

```
/* Enforce table width */
.fixed { table-layout: fixed; }
```

A fixed table layout has the added benefit that the browser can render the table more quickly because it knows the dimension of the table as soon as the first row is received.

CHAPTER 25

Media

CSS provides a way to present documents differently, depending on the device on which they are viewed. Such conditional style rules are placed within a media rule, which consists of @media, followed by an expression that limits the scope and a set of curly brackets that encloses the conditional style rules.

```
@media screen {
  /* screen devices only */
}
```

Media Types

The media type condition, which was introduced in CSS 2, lists the following valid values, including the default value all for targeting all device types:

```
all | aural | braille | handheld | print | projection | screen |
tty | tv | embossed
```

Unfortunately, the media type does not tell much about the device, so it is seldom used for its intended purpose. Modern smartphones, tablets, laptops, and desktop computers all identify themselves as screen types.

© Mikael Olsson 2019
M. Olsson, *CSS3 Quick Syntax Reference*, https://doi.org/10.1007/978-1-4842-4903-1_25

The main use of the media type condition today is to differentiate between onscreen and printed documents to enable more print-friendly document formatting.

```
/* Print only */
@media print
{
  /* Hide navigation */
  #navigation { display: none; }

  /* Start h1 elements on a new page */
  h1 { page-break-before: always; }
}
```

Media rules are typically placed at the bottom of the style sheet, which allows the cascade to override the rules defined earlier. If the style sheet contains a lot of conditional rules, it might be preferable to move them to a separate style sheet that is included after the primary style sheet. The media condition can then be specified with the media attribute on the <link> element.

```
<link rel="stylesheet" media="print" href="myprint.css">
```

This style sheet contains the print condition, so it is applied only when the document is sent to print media. Keep in mind that browsers still download a style sheet, even if its media condition is false.

Media Queries

CSS 3 went a step. farther by allowing media rules to target the capabilities of the device, not just its type. It introduced a wide range of media features that can be targeted, as seen in the following list. All these features, except for orientation, grid, and scan, can be prefixed with min- or max- to define constraints.

```
width | height | device-width | device-height | aspect-ratio |
device-aspect-ratio | resolution | orientation | color | color-
index | monochrome
```

The most important media features, min-width and max-width, allow you to create responsive designs in which the site layout changes based on the viewport of the device's browser.

A media query combines a media type and a condition consisting of one or more media features. For example, the rules within the following media query are applied only when viewed on screen-based media with a minimum width of 600 pixels:

```
@media screen and (min-width: 600px) {}
```

Media queries are case-insensitive, and parentheses around the condition are required. The and operator seen here is used to combine the media type and the media feature, but it can also combine multiple media features together:

```
@media (max-width: 500px) and (min-aspect-ratio: 1/1) {}
```

This media query. is true if the viewing device has a max width of 500 pixels and at least a 1:1 aspect ratio (square or landscape viewport). Notice that the media type is left out here, so the rule applies to all media types.

Logical Operators

In addition to the logical and operator, media queries can include the logical not and only operators as well as the logical or operation. The comma (,) is used as the or operator to separate groups of multiple queries. The following media rule is true if either the screen is at least 700 pixels wide or if the device is in landscape mode:

```
@media (min-width: 700px), (orientation: landscape) {}
```

The not operator is used to negate an entire media query. It cannot negate an individual feature. For example, the following media rule applies only if the device screen is not 800 pixels wide:

```
@media not screen and (device-width: 800px) {}
```

The only operator was added to hide media queries from older browsers. According to the specification, browsers that do not support media queries should interpret the following rule as being applied to the only media type, which is invalid and thereby causes the conditional style rules to be ignored.

```
/* Not applied in older browsers */
@media only screen and (min-width: 600px) {}
```

Regrettably, IE 6-8 did not implement the specification correctly. The media query is therefore ignored even if the only keyword is left out, instead of then applying the media rule to all screen-based devices.

```
/* Not applied in IE 6-8 */
@media screen and (min-width : 600px) {}
```

Note that both the not and only operators require the use of an explicit media type, whereas the logical or (,) and logical and operators do not.

Support for media queries has become widespread in all major browsers. The min-width and max-width queries, for example, are supported in Chrome 1+, Firefox 3.5+, Safari 4+, Opera 8+, and IE 9+.

Testing Media Queries

It is important to test your media queries to make sure that your site looks good in as many devices as possible. The latest web browsers all re-evaluate media queries as the browser environment is changed (when the window is resized, for example). You can therefore test how your design responds to different device dimensions just by resizing your browser window. Chrome also has a built-in toolbar for testing how your site will look on different devices. To show the device selection toolbar first bring up the Inspect window (Ctrl+Shift+I) and then click the Toggle device toolbar icon in the upper left corner (Ctrl+Shift+M).

Responsive Design Guidelines

When designing a responsive layout, it is often easiest to start with the mobile layout first and define how it looks without any media rules. As you expand the viewport, notice when this layout ceases to look good. This is the breakpoint at which you should change the part of the layout that visually breaks or ceases to be useful. This change might include adding a second column or changing to a more advanced navigation menu. You define these breakpoints using the min-width and max-width media features to override styles as the viewport gets larger, as shown in the following example. Continue this method of finding breakpoints until you reach a high enough resolution. Depending on your layout, you might need to define only a few breakpoints.

```
@media (min-width: 800px) {
  body { background: red; }
}
@media (min-width: 401px) and (max-width: 799px) {
  body { background: green; }
}
@media (max-width: 400px) {
  body { background: blue; }
}
```

CHAPTER 26

Layout

There are many ways to create a layout in CSS. This chapter will look at some of these methods and how they compare when creating a simple layout.

Float

In the early days of CSS one of the few available methods for creating a grid-like design was to use the float property to get block elements to stay on the same line.

```
.left { float: left; }
.clear { clear: both; }
```

To show the effect of floating elements the following box style will be used.

```
.box {
  width: 100px;
  height: 100px;
  margin: 1em;
  background: #ccc;
}
```

© Mikael Olsson 2019
M. Olsson, *CSS3 Quick Syntax Reference*, https://doi.org/10.1007/978-1-4842-4903-1_26

Clearing issues and browser inconsistencies aside, the float property provided a non-intuitive way of defining a layout which has since long been deprecated as better methods became available. The floating layout defined here is illustrated in Figure 26-1.

```
<div class="left box"></div>
<div class="left box"></div>
<div class="clear"></div>
<div class="left box"></div>
<div class="left box"></div>
<div class="clear"></div>
```

Inline-Block

The inline-block display type offered several advantages compared with floating layouts, including greater simplicity and no need for clearing floats. Moreover, the layout won't break when elements have different heights as they would with floating elements. The vertical-align property can be used to specify how elements align when their heights differ.

```
.inline {
  display: inline-block;
  vertical-align: top;
}
```

An issue with inline-block elements is that any whitespace around elements will be visible as gaps. Removing the whitespace, or moving the end tags around as seen here, solves the issue but makes the HTML less readable. The example given here produces the same result as seen in Figure 26-1.

```
<div>
  <div class="inline box">
  </div><div class="inline box"></div>
</div>
<div>
  <div class="inline box">
  </div><div class="inline box"></div>
</div>
```

Figure 26-1. *Floating layout*

Multiple Columns

The multi-column layout allows content to flow into multiple columns, as in a newspaper. It is enabled by setting one or both of the following properties: column-count and column-width. The column-count property specifies the number of columns the content will break into, letting the browser divide their width equally. Conversely, the column-width property sets the fixed width of all columns, leaving the browser to work out how many columns will fit based on available screen width.

```
.flexible-cols {
  column-count: 3;
}
```

```
.fixed-cols {
  column-width: 14em;
}
```

Column boxes cannot be targeted individually in CSS so all columns must be the same size. A vertical line can be added between columns using the column-rule property, which behaves like the border property. The gap between columns can also be adjusted using the column-gap property. It can be changed to any valid length unit and is 1em by default.

```
.mycols {
  column-gap: 2em;
  column-rule: 1px solid #ccc
}
```

Support for the multi-column properties is available in Chrome 50+, Firefox 50+, Safari 10+, Opera 37+, and IE 10+. The -webkit- and -moz-prefixes can be used to extend support to Chrome 4+, Firefox 2+, Safari 3.1+, and Opera 11.5+.

Flexbox

The flexible box or flexbox module provides a simple way to create a fluid layout in one dimension, either a horizontal row or a vertical column. To enable the flexbox layout the flex display property is applied to the container element, called the flex container.

```
.flex-wrapper {
  display: flex;
}
```

Child elements of this container are called flex items. They are by default laid out according to text direction (typically left to right) in a row in the order they appear in the source document. Consider the following flex items.

```
.item1 {
  flex-grow: 1;
  flex-shrink: 1;
  flex-basis: 10em
}
.item2 {
  flex-grow: 3;
  flex-shrink: 2;
  flex-basis: 10em
}
```

The flex-basis property specifies that both items want to be 10em wide. Because of the flex-grow property, if the flex container is larger than 20em the second item will take up three times as much of the surplus space as the first item. In contrast, if the container shrinks to less than 20em width the second item will contract twice as much as the first item, as specified by the flex-shrink property. All three of these properties are normally defined using the flex shorthand property to make sure all values are set.

```
flex (flex): 0 1 auto | flex-grow + flex-shrink + flex-basis
```

If the space of the container becomes too narrow to fit the item's flex-basis setting the container can be made to wrap to another row using the flex-wrap property.

```
flex-wrap (flex): nowrap | wrap | wrap-reverse
```

Each new row (or column) will become a new flex container distributing the space between items that wrap to that container. Items wrapped to the second row will not align with items on the first row.

```
.flex-wrapper {
  display: flex;
  flex-wrap: wrap;
}
```

Placed within the flex container these items will be evenly distributed on the horizontal axis even if the browser is resized, without any need for media queries, as seen in Figure 22-1.

```
<div class="flex-wrapper">
  <div class="item1 box"></div>
  <div class="item2 box"></div>
</div>
```

Flex items are by default laid out horizontally in the text direction in the order they appear in the source document. The direction of the flex container is determined by the flex-direction property, which can have one of four different values.

```
flex-direction (flex): row | row-reverse | column | column-
reverse
```

Individual items can also be targeted to change their order using the order property, which is a unitless number that starts at 0 for the first item. When used together with media queries this can allow for items to be reshuffled if needed based on available screen size.

```
.item2 {
  /* Position before item1 */
  order: -1;
}
```

A feature of flexbox is that it becomes easy to properly align items using the align-items, align-self, align-content, and justify-content properties.

```
align-items (flex): stretch | flex-start | flex-end | center |
baseline
align-self (flex): auto | flex-start | flex-end | center |
baseline | stretch
```

The align-items property sets the main-axis alignment of all direct child flexbox items, which refers to vertical-alignment for horizontal flex boxes. This setting can be overridden on individual items using the align-self property.

```
.flex-wrapper {
  display: flex;
  /* Vertically align items to top */
  align-items: start;
}
.item1 {
  /* Stretch auto-sized item to container height */
  align-self: stretch;
}
```

Alignment of the secondary axis, which means horizontal alignment for a horizontal flexbox, is done using the justify-content property.

```
justify-content (flex): flex-start | flex-end | center | space-
between | space-around | space-evenly
```

This property is applied to the flex container and affects all items.

```
.flex-wrapper {
  display: flex;
  /* Center items vertically */
  align-items: center;
```

```
  /* Center items horizontally */
  justify-content: center;
}
```

Lastly, the align-content property specifies how a flex containers lines will align when there is extra space available on the secondary axis. This will only have an effect when there are multiple lines in a flex container.

```
align-content: stretch | flex-start | flex-end | center |
space-between | space-around
```

Each line height would by default stretch and be distributed evenly on the secondary axis, but the align-content property can change this behavior to for instance grouping the lines together in the middle of the flex container.

```
.flex-wrapper {
  display: flex;
  height: 100vh;
  flex-wrap: wrap;
  /* Align rows in center */
  align-content: center;
}
```

The flexbox properties are supported in all modern browsers, including: Chrome 29+, Firefox 22+, Safari 10+, Opera 48+, and IE 11+.

Grid Box

The grid module was designed for two-dimensional layouts, when there's a need to control the layout by both row and column. Whereas a flexbox can adjust the number of items per row according to available space, the

grid will always have the specified number of columns and rows. To start
defining a grid layout the display value is set to grid. As with flexbox, this
changes all direct children of the container into grid items.

```
.grid-wrapper {
  display: grid;
}
```

This will default to a one column grid, so the following items will look
the same as they would in the normal flow with a single column and two
rows.

```
<div class="grid-wrapper">
  <div class="box"></div>
  <div class="box"></div>
</div>
```

A grid layout can be either implicitly or explicitly defined. This grid
here is implicit, because the number of rows and columns are not explicitly
defined. The height of such rows can be set with the grid-auto-rows
property.

grid-auto-rows (grid): auto | max-content | min-content |
length

More columns can be added using the grid-template-columns
property, with each specified value defining the size of a column as either a
length value or a percentage.

```
.grid-wrapper {
  display: grid;
  grid-template-columns: 100px 100px;
  grid-auto-rows: 100px;
}
```

If an item taller than the row height is added, its content will overflow. To instead get a flexible height that expands to fit the content the minmax function can be used. This function sets the minimum and maximum height of a row (or width of a column) so that it can adjust automatically to the height of the content. The function can be used with the following grid properties: grid-template-columns, grid-template-rows, grid-auto-columns, and grid-auto-rows.

```
grid-auto-rows: minmax(100px, auto);
```

An explicit number of rows can be defined using the grid-template-rows property. Keep in mind that any items placed outside of an explicitly defined grid will automatically expand the grid.

```
grid-template-rows (grid): none | auto | max-content | min-
content | length
```

One way to specify the size of a grid row or column is using the fractional unit denoted by fl. This unit represents a fraction of the available space in the grid container, so the following grid layout will have two rows with the first one taking up 40% of the available space and the second one taking up the remaining 60%. Note the repeat function used here as a simple way to specify four columns of equal width. It gives the same result as specifying the value auto four times.

```
.grid-wrapper {
  display: grid;
  height: 100vh;
  grid-template-rows: 2fr 3fr;
  grid-template-columns: repeat(4, 1fr);
}
```

There is a shorthand property named grid-template available for setting the grid-template properties all at once.

grid-template (grid): none | grid-template-rows / grid-template-columns | grid-template-areas

The following specifies a grid layout with two columns and one row with a 200px height.

```
.grid-wrapper {
  display: grid;
  grid-template: 200px / auto auto
}
```

Notice that the grid-template property has a possible value called grid-template-areas. This property provides an alternative way to define the grid layout by first naming the individual items with the grid-area property. The names can then be referenced to position them on the grid using the grid-template-areas property, as seen here. Keep in mind that an element can take up more than one cell on the grid.

```
.item1 { grid-area: header; }
.item2 { grid-area: menu; }
.item3 { grid-area: content; }
.item4 { grid-area: footer; }

.grid-wrapper {
  display: grid;
  grid-template-areas:
  'header header header'  /* row 1 */
  'menu content content'  /* row 2 */
  'footer footer footer'; /* row 3 */
}
```

Items normally appear on the grid in the order they are listed in the HTML. This placement can be changed using the grid-column and grid-row properties to designate where an item will appear. For example, the following styling places the header element so that it takes up the first two cells of the grid on the first row.

```
header {
  grid-column: 1 / 2;
  grid-row: 1;
}
```

Support for the grid layout properties is available in: Chrome 57+, Firefox 52+, Safari 10.1+, Opera 44+, and Edge 16+.

CHAPTER 27

Best Practices

You now have an understanding of the fundamentals of CSS. This final chapter takes a step back to look at good coding practices and standards for style sheet development. Following these guidelines can help you write robust CSS code that is easy to maintain, reuse, and extend upon.

Reusable Code

A key idea to a manageable style sheet is to avoid duplicate code. Classes help achieve this goal because they are reusable and can be combined in different ways, giving you a flexible design that is easy to evolve.

Any time you find page items that share style properties, you should consider combining those repeating patterns. This makes it easier to reuse and update the code as well as to maintain style consistency on the site. Consider the following simple example:

```css
.module {
  width: 200px;
  border: 1px solid #ccc;
  border-radius: 3px;
}
.widget {
  width: 300px;
  border: 1px solid #ccc;
  border-radius: 3px;
}
```

© Mikael Olsson 2019
M. Olsson, *CSS3 Quick Syntax Reference*, https://doi.org/10.1007/978-1-4842-4903-1_27

These classes have two styles in common that can be moved into a third class to avoid unnecessary repetition. This process makes the classes more generic and therefore more reusable.

```
.box-border {
  border: 1px solid #ccc;
  border-radius: 3px;
}
.module { width: 200px; }
.widget { width: 300px; }
```

When optimizing classes for reuse, it is important to consider their size. The goal is to find the middle ground between classes that are not too broad or too narrow. Too-broad classes lead to unnecessary repetition; too-narrow classes make it difficult to change the design.

Global Modifiers

There are certain style properties that are very commonly used. Instead of adding these styles to every other class, it is sometimes better to create a general class with that single style, which you can then apply to the elements that need it. For example, floating elements to the left or right is such a common operation. These styles are well suited as global modifiers.

```
.left  { float: left; }
.right { float: right; }
```

When you want an element floated to the right or left, you can simply add one of these classes to the element:

```
<div class="left">...</div>
```

Global modifiers such as these can be very useful when just a single style property is needed. However, you should avoid combining more than a few of them because it can become difficult to adjust your design if all page items are composed of such small classes.

Style Sheet Structure

By organizing your style sheets, you can make it easier for yourself and other developers to quickly understand the structure of your CSS. The larger a site becomes, and the more developers are involved, the greater is the need to keep things well organized. But it is good practice to always keep your style sheets well structured, regardless of the size of the web site.

The top portion of a style sheet usually includes information about the file and its author. This metadata should include the author's name and contact information. This way, if any questions come up about the document, the developer currently working on the site knows whom to ask. Other potentially useful metadata includes the file's creation date, last modified date, version number, title, and description.

```
/*
 * Title: My Theme
 * Version: 1.2.3
 * Author: My Name
 */
```

As for the style rules, they should be grouped into sections, and each section should be labeled with a distinguishing comment. This grouping and labeling enables you to find what you need much more quickly. The sections you need depend on the site, but here are some example sections:

```
/* === Normalization === */
/* === Primary layout === */
/* === Secondary layout === */
```

```
/* === Tertiary layout === */
/* === Navigation === */
/* === Text-related === */
/* === Links and images === */
/* === General styles === */
/* === General classes === */
/* === Miscellaneous === */
```

The equal signs after the section name help visually distinguish the sections from other comments. They also act as a marker that you can search for to easily traverse the sections.

With large style sheets, the section names can be listed as a table of contents below the metadata, which makes it easier for developers to get an overview of how the file is organized.

```
/* Table of Contents
   -----------------
   Normalization
   Primary layout (body, primary divs)
   Secondary layout (header, footer, sidebar)
   Tertiary layout (page regions)
   Navigation (menus)
   Text-related (paragraphs, headings, lists)
   Links and images
   General styles (forms, tables, etc.)
   General classes (.clear, .center, etc.)
   Miscellaneous
*/
```

Within each section, you should declare your most generic rules first, followed by rules with increasing specificity. Your elements can inherit styles, and it is easier for you to override specific styles when needed.

Another thing to consider is how to structure properties within a rule. A popular approach is to group the properties according to type. You do not have to label the groups as in the following example, but it helps if you keep the groups in the same order throughout your style sheet. Doing so enables you to more quickly scan through the rules in search of specific properties.

```css
.myclass {
  /* Positioning */
  position: absolute;
  top: 0;
  right: 0;

  /* Box model */
  display: inline-block;
  width: 100px;
  height: 100px;

  /* Color */
  background: #ccc;
  color: #fff;

  /* Text */
  font-size: 1em;
  line-height: 1.2;
  text-align: right;

  /* Other */
  cursor: pointer;
}
```

Keep in mind that these are only guidelines; choose a structure that works for you and aim to keep it consistent.

Naming Conventions

It is helpful to name classes and ids in a way that clarifies their intended use. This structural naming convention means that the name should describe what the class or id is used for instead of what it looks like or where it is used in the web document.

The advantage of this naming convention is that it becomes easier to change the look of your web site. For example, naming an id container #main-content is better than naming it #center-column-500px. In addition to intuitively understanding the use of the id, the first name is more versatile in case you later need to adjust the position or size of the element it is applied to.

```
#main-content {
  width: 500px;
  margin: 0 auto; /* centered */
}
```

Names should be semantic, but not so semantic that they limit reuse. For instance, naming a class .header-top-margin is not as flexible as naming the class .small-top-margin (or .small-tm). To later recall that the class is mainly used in the header is easy enough; for example, you can search for the class name using the search function when viewing the page source in a web browser.

```
.small-top-margin { margin-top: 1em; }
```

In addition to conveying intended use, the class name can also show its relationships to other classes. For example, if a container class is called .post, the title for that container can be named .post-title to show that the class should be used only within an element applying the .post class.

```
.post {
  margin: 1em 0;
}
  .post-title {
    font-size: 1.2em;
  }
```

The title class could also have been written as `.post.title` to ensure that the `.title` class can be used only within a container using the `.post` class. However, the `.post-title` name helps avoid naming conflicts and does not increase specificity, so that naming convention is often preferable. Notice that the relationship between the rules is further emphasized using indentation, which can significantly improve the code's readability.

Normalization

Different browsers render some elements slightly differently, mainly because of variations in their default style sheets. To get a shared baseline, it is common to include a group of rules that normalize these browser inconsistencies and set reasonable defaults. The most popular choice for this is the GitHub `Normalize.css` project.[1] By including these rules at the top of your style sheet (or a subset of them per your site's requirements), you have a consistent starting point across all browsers from which you can build. The `Normalize.css` style sheet includes ample comments that explain each browser inconsistency that it resolves.

---

[1]http://necolas.github.io/normalize.css/

Debugging

There are many useful debugging tools available that can significantly simplify your work as a web developer. Chrome and Firefox for instance have built-in browser support to debug CSS, HTML and JavaScript live on any web page for testing purposes. To take advantage of this you bring up the development tools window using the shortcut Ctrl+Shift+I on Windows or Cmd+Opt+I on Mac.

Alternatively, you can right-click an element on a page and select Inspect Element to bring up the same window in element inspection mode. One of the features of this window is to discover exactly which styles apply to a selected element and how the element changes if you toggle specific styles on or off. To get even more sophisticated tools for debugging and web development you can download the Developer Edition of the Firefox browser.[2]

Validation

It is a good idea to check that your CSS complies with the W3C standard. Improper code may cause unexpected results in how your site appears in different browsers. Moreover, having error-free code is a sign of a quality web site.

The W3C provides its own online tool for validating CSS.[3] It checks a submitted page and returns any errors and warnings found on the page for you to fix. It also has a similar tool for validating HTML documents,[4] which is just as important to do. To make validation even more

---

[2]www.mozilla.org/en-US/firefox/developer/
[3]http://jigsaw.w3.org/css-validator/
[4]http://validator.w3.org

convenient, you can download a browser plug-in that checks the page's code for you, such as the Web Developer plug-in available on Chrome, Firefox, and Opera.[5]

Single Style Sheet

For performance reasons, it is best to include a site's style rules in a single external style sheet. Doing so minimizes the number of HTTP requests necessary to load the web site, while allowing the CSS file to be cached so that the visitor's browser has to download it only once.

During development of a large site, it is often preferable to separate style rules into several more manageable CSS files. To have the best of both worlds, these development files can be combined into a single file as part of the site's build process, using a CSS preprocessor.

Preprocessor

As a website grows so too does its style sheet and it can quickly reach a point when the style sheet becomes difficult to overview and maintain. A way to reduce complexity of large style sheets is to use a CSS preprocessor, such as SASS.[6] The preprocessor perceivably extends the CSS language with basic programming features, such as variables, loops, conditions, and functions. This allows you to better organize the style sheet and make use of reusable components to achieve greater results with less code. Note that preprocessors do not extend the CSS standard itself. The style sheets in the extended syntax are processed by a program and turned into regular CSS style sheets.

---

[5]http://chrispederick.com/work/web-developer/
[6]https://sass-lang.com

Minification

Minification is the process of removing unnecessary characters from code to reduce its size. When a CSS file is minified, whitespace characters are removed, and the rules are optimized and restructured to load more quickly. This compression can greatly reduce the size of the file, which improves site performance at the cost of code readability. Because of the reduced readability, it is preferable to work with the uncompressed style sheet and have the minification step repeated whenever the CSS file is updated. Minification can be done automatically using the CSS preprocessor mentioned earlier or manually with an online tool such as Clean CSS.[7]

One optimization that minification tools cannot do is to find and remove unused CSS rules. A useful Firefox plug-in that can help you perform this task is Dust-Me Selectors.[8] This plug-in can test pages individually and also scan through an entire site in search of unused selectors.

Cross-Browser Testing

Even with your code normalized and validated, there can still be some differences in the way a web page is rendered in various browsers, especially in older versions. It is therefore necessary to test your site in all the browser versions you want your site to support.

To make this testing process easier, you can use BrowserStack,[9] which is an online tool for checking browser compatibility. It shows you how your site will look on different versions of the browsers you select. You can also see how your site will look on mobile devices and tablets.

---

[7]www.cleancss.com

[8]www.brothercake.com/dustmeselectors/

[9]www.browserstack.com/screenshots

Index

A

Absolute units, 47
align-content property, 160
align-items property, 159
Attribute selector, 13
    delimited value, 14
    end value, 15
    language, 14
    start value, 15
    substring value, 14

B

background property, 76–77
background-attachment property, 72
background-clip property, 75
background-color property, 71
background-image property, 71–72
background-origin property, 75–76
background-position property, 73
background-repeat property, 72
background-size property, 74–75
Border properties
    border-color, 97–98
    border-radius, 99–100
    border-style, 95–96
    border-width, 97
    subproperties, 98

Box model, CSS
    block elements, 90–91
    inline elements, 90–91
    <span> and <div> elements, 91
    semantic elements, 92
box-shadow property, 61

C

calc function, 52
Classification properties
    clear, 133
    cursor, 134–135
    display, 129–131
    float, 132–133
    opacity, 131–132
    visibility, 131
Class selector, 9
clip property, 118–119
Colors
    hexadecimal notation, 43–44
    HSLA notation, 46
    HSL notation, 45–46
    named notation, 43
    RGBA notation, 45
    RGB notation, 44
    short hexadecimal notation, 44
Comments, 4–5
Cross-browser testing process, 174

Printed in the United States
By Bookmasters